Stargazing

The sociology of fame and celebrity is at the cutting edge of current scholarship in a number of different areas of study. *Stargazing* highlights the interactional dynamics of celebrity and fame in contemporary society, including the thoughts and feelings of stars on the red carpet, the thrills and risks of encountering a famous person at a convention or on the streets, and the excitement generated even by the obvious fakery of celebrity impersonators. Using compelling, real-life examples involving popular celebrities, Ferris and Harris examine how the experience and meanings of celebrity are shaped by social norms, interactional negotiations, and interpretive storytelling.

Kerry O. Ferris is associate professor of Sociology at Northern Illinois University. She works toward a sociology of fame using ethnographic methods and a symbolic-interactionist approach. Her work has been published in *Symbolic Interaction*, *Journal of Contemporary Ethnography*, and *Human Studies*. Her current project examines small-market newscasters' experiences of local celebrity.

Scott R. Harris is associate professor at Saint Louis University. His research centers on social interaction and social constructionism. His books include *What Is Constructionism? Navigating Its Use in Sociology* (Lynne Rienner 2010) and *The Meanings of Marital Equality* (SUNY 2006).

Contemporary Sociological Perspectives

Edited by **Valerie Jenness**, University of California, Irvine
and **Jodi O'Brien**, Seattle University

This innovative series is for all readers interested in books that provide frameworks for making sense of the complexities of contemporary social life. Each of the books in this series uses a sociological lens to provide current critical and analytical perspectives on significant social issues, patterns and trends. The series consists of books that integrate the best ideas in sociological thought with an aim toward public education and engagement. These books are designed for use in the classroom as well as for scholars and socially-curious general readers.

Published:

Political Justice and Religious Values by Charles F. Andrain
GIS and Spatial Analysis for the Social Sciences by Robert Nash Parker and Emily K. Asencio
Hoop Dreams on Wheels: Disability and the Competitive Wheelchair Athlete
   by Ronald J. Berger
The Internet and Social Inequalities by James C. Witte and Susan E. Mannon
Media and Middle Class Mom: Images and Realities of Work and Family
   by Lara Descartes and Conrad Kottak
Watching TV Is Not Required: Thinking about Media and Thinking about Thinking
   by Bernard McGrane and John Gunderson
Violence Against Women: Vulnerable Populations by Douglas Brownridge
State of Sex: Tourism, Sex and Sin in the New American Heartland
   by Barbara G. Brents, Crystal A. Jackson and Kate Hausbeck
Social Statistics: The Basics and Beyond by Thomas J. Linneman
Sociologists Backstage: Answers to 10 Questions about What They Do
   by Sarah Fenstermaker and Nikki Jones
Gender Circuits by Eve Shapiro

Forthcoming:

Transform Yourself, Transform the World: A Practical Guide to Women's and Gender Studies
   by Michele Berger and Cheryl Radeloff
Surviving Dictatorship: Visual and Social Representations by Jacqueline Adams
Social Theory: Classical and Contemporary Perspectives by Wesley Longhofer
Sociology Looks at the Arts by Julia Rothenberg
The Womanist Idea by Layli Phillips Maparyan

Stargazing

Celebrity, Fame, and Social Interaction

Kerry O. Ferris

Northern Illinois University

Scott R. Harris

Saint Louis University

Routledge
Taylor & Francis Group

NEW YORK AND LONDON

First published 2011
by Routledge
270 Madison Avenue, New York, NY 10016

Simultaneously published in the UK
by Routledge
2 Park Square, Milton Park, Abingdon, Oxon OX14 4RN

Routledge is an imprint of the Taylor & Francis Group, an informa business

The right of Kerry O. Ferris and Scott R. Harris to be identified as authors of this work has been asserted by them in accordance with sections 77 and 78 of the Copyright, Designs and Patents Act 1988.

Typeset in Adobe Caslon and Copperplate Gothic by
RefineCatch Limited, Bungay, Suffolk, UK
Printed and bound in the United States of America on acid-free paper by
Walsworth Publishing Company, Marceline, MO

Library of Congress Cataloging in Publication Data
Ferris, Kerry.
   Stargazing : celebrity, fame, and social interaction / Kerry O. Ferris,
Scott R. Harris
      p. cm. (Contemporary sociological perspectives)
   ISBN 978–0–415–88427–3 (hbk.)—ISBN 978–0–415–88428–0 (pbk.)
   ISBN 978–0–203–83134–2 (ebook)   1. Fame—Social aspects.
   2. Celebrities.   I. Harris, Scott R., 1969 Sept. 16–   II. Title.
   BJ1470.5.F47 2011
   302'.1—dc22

                                                    2010032826

ISBN13: 978–0–415–88427–3 (hbk)
ISBN13: 978–0–415–88428–0 (pbk)
ISBN13: 978–0–203–83134–2 (ebk)

SUSTAINABLE
FORESTRY
INITIATIVE
Certified Chain of Custody
Promoting Sustainable
Forest Management
www.sfiprogram.org
NSF-SFI-COC-C0004285
The SFI label applies to the text stock.

TABLE OF CONTENTS

TABLE OF CONTENTS

SERIES FOREWORD

As its title suggests, *Stargazing* is a book about looking at stars! The look is through the lens of a sociological perspective and the stars are celebrities. By utilizing a microsociological perspective to make sense of modern day celebrity and our relationship to those the media render highly visible and (seemingly) newsworthy in our celebrity culture, this book provides compelling sociological answers to a slew of interesting questions: Why do people take an interest in the lives of celebrities? Why do we tolerate law-bending paparazzi behavior that we perhaps wouldn't tolerate from others? Why are the majority of the magazines at the check-out stand hawking voyeurism? Why do people look even if we don't want to? Why do people pay to look at impersonators of celebrities? Why does fame sometimes provoke obsession?

To address these interesting questions, Ferris and Harris provide a detailed analysis of celebrity-focused interactions, such as the thrills and the risks of fans' contact with the famous, the fun of watching celebrity impersonators perform, and the phenomena known as "celebrity stalking." Beyond the fun of reading about celebrity and our relationship to it in a social context in which fame is a commodity, this book provides an example of symbolic interaction in action. Ferris and Harris deftly draw on accessible examples and rich data to make sociological sense of how meaning-making occurs through real and imagined engagement with celebrities; more generally, the focus is on norms, negotiations, discourse, and recurring generic social processes that cut across many types of social interactions. The result is a compelling assessment of celebrity that simultaneously serves to demystify fame and our relationship to it, demonstrates the application of the sociological imagination, and renders visible social processes and structures that create lived realities we so often take for granted.

Valerie Jenness
Jodi O'Brien
Series Editors

PREFACE

Stargazing is intended to provide a succinct, interesting, and rigorous look at the interactional dynamics of different aspects of celebrity in contemporary society, including the thoughts and feelings of celebrities on the red carpet, the thrills and risks of celebrity sightings and fan–celebrity contact, and the excitement generated even by obvious fakes (celebrity impersonators).

The book is disciplinarily-grounded in Sociology while also drawing from and addressing disciplines such as communications, cultural studies, and psychology. *Stargazing* contributes to the literature by directing attention to the meanings of celebrity and fame that are created in face-to-face social interaction.

Academic interest in celebrity has increased in recent years. However, as we explain in Chapter 1, many existing works tend to either pathologize or commodify the phenomenon of celebrity—focusing on the dysfunctions of fame as well as its connection to economic exploitation. In contrast, *Stargazing* will focus on social interaction and the meanings of celebrity from the perspectives of those who enact and consume it.

No group of scholars can claim ownership of the topic of "meaning." Research from the perspective of cultural studies, for example, makes matters of interpretation a central concern. But as sociologists of interaction we focus in more nuanced detail on the construction of meaning that occurs in face-to-face and mediated social interaction.

We wrote *Stargazing* as a text that could be used in courses on Social Psychology, Social Interaction, or Popular Culture. Instructors could also assign *Stargazing* as a supplementary reading in Introduction to Sociology, or in other courses where there is a need to give students an accessible example of "microsociology" or "symbolic interactionism." In addition, some readers may appreciate the book merely out of personal interest. A large number of people in the U.S. and around the world are avid celebrity observers. For these fans and critics of the famous, *Stargazing* may provide a fascinating look at celebrity that goes deeper than coverage in the mass media—without becoming too ponderous.

OVERVIEW

In Chapter 1, we provide an introduction to the Sociology of celebrity and fame, a relatively young field that does have some identifiable roots in classical theory. While the topic has been relatively ignored by sociologists for many decades, it has recently been taken up by both theorists and empirical researchers in Sociology and a variety of related fields. We identify two major themes—"celebrity as pathology" and "celebrity as commodity"—that currently dominate the literature. Briefly put, celebrity has been approached as a matter of individual and group dysfunction or as a matter of exploitation and mass marketing. While work in these veins has much to offer, we argue that more attention could be given to meaning-oriented research that reflects the lived experiences of those who swim in the sea of celebrity culture everyday. What does celebrity mean to those who produce it, consume it, engage with it and live it? If more researchers take up these questions, then the sociology of celebrity could become an even more vibrant and vigorous area of study. The subsequent chapters take up the issues of meaning and interaction in more depth, examining celebrity and fame as they are constructed in face-to-face and mediated settings.

Chapter 2 focuses on the dynamics of fan–celebrity encounters. Fans of serial television—such as soap opera and science fiction shows—can take their hobbies very seriously. This chapter examines the activities through which certain fans seek face-to-face encounters with the celebrities they admire, and how this intersection of the ordinary with the extraordinary creates problems of interpretation that fans attempt to solve. Fans make and take advantage of opportunities for pre-staged encounters at official public appearances by their favorite actors. Some fans may also encounter their favorite celebrities by chance in the course of their daily rounds in "celebrity sightings" or unstaged encounters. Certain fans, however, actively pursue actors, deliberately seeking them out and creating fan-staged encounters. These efforts produce a distinctive interactional tension in which pursuing fans recognize the similarities between their behavior and that of "celebrity stalkers," and attempt to differentiate themselves from the stalkers that celebrities fear.

Compared to pre-staged and fan-staged encounters, celebrity sightings are unpredictable and serendipitous events. Yet even these relatively unusual and rare happenings are socially patterned, at least from a *microstructuralist* perspective. In Chapter 3, we argue that there is a "moral order" to celebrity sightings. Both fan and celebrity behavior seems governed, or at least strongly influenced, by social norms. Fans report feeling an obligation to invoke a distinctive version of the norm of civil inattention when they encounter famous individuals in public places—in other words, they feel they must pretend that they haven't noticed the famous person in their path. And when fans cannot contain their enthusiasm and do approach a celebrity, they often provide "accounts" (either to the star or to others after the fact) that attempt to excuse or justify their behavior. At the same time, fans hold stars accountable for not doing their part to support the norm of civil inattention (e.g., fans condemn celebrities who draw unnecessary attention to themselves).

Human beings are reality *negotiators* as well as rule followers, as their "accounts" arguably imply. In Chapter 4, we give closer attention to the negotiations and definitional balancing acts which performers and fans can engage in, by focusing on celebrity impersonators. Impersonators and their audiences collaborate to produce an intelligible encounter where the real and the unreal coexist comfortably. Successful shows seem to require that impersonators and fans find a workable balance between several layers of meaning, including the contradictory ideas that the person on stage is and is not the star, is the celebrity and is a particular character the celebrity once played, and so on.

Social order, or the appearance thereof, is produced by interaction, norms, and spontaneous negotiations. It is also produced by talk. In Chapters 5 and 6 of *Stargazing*, we focus more closely on language while turning towards the perspectives of celebrities themselves. The difficulties of access prevent us from directly interviewing stars, but we can record, transcribe, and analyze the interviews that stars frequently give on the red carpet just prior to award shows. Each year, before the Oscars, Grammies, Golden Globes, and other award shows, celebrities are asked how it feels to be nominated, what it was like to work with a famous director, whether they always knew their film or album would be a success, and other related questions. These chapters turn a close eye to these red-carpet comments, treating them as interpretive claims-making rather than mere reality reports. A *discursive* perspective allows us to ask critical questions about the meanings that celebrities' comments create and the purposes their answers may serve.

While it is sometimes tempting to be cynical or harsh towards celebrities, it is also possible to treat their behavior as just another manifestation of practices that occur in other realms of society, including extraordinary and mundane settings. (For example, in our everyday lives, we too are asked to explain when we first knew we would be a psychology major, how we feel about graduating, and so on.) Throughout *Stargazing*, and especially in our conclusion in Chapter 7, we highlight the parallels that can be drawn between celebrity-centered and non-celebrity-centered interaction. The perspectives of microstructuralism, negotiated order, and discourse analysis have generated insights and concepts that can be applied to any interactional setting. We argue that research in the area of celebrity and fame can borrow from, and contribute to, this body of work.

ACKNOWLEDGMENTS

We both express our appreciation to the production staff at Routledge, to our editor Steve Rutter for his enthusiastic interest, and to Valerie Jenness, Jodi O'Brien, and Brad Wright for their comments and reviews. Scott is also grateful to Jenine Harris for her daily support and encouragement. Kerry would like to thank Greg Wennerdahl for always believing that whatever she writes is pure genius—even if he hasn't read it yet!

Earlier versions of some chapters were previously published as journal articles. We thank the following presses for their permission to re-use our work.

Chapter 1 is based on the article "The Sociology of Celebrity." *Sociology Compass* 1(1):371–384, by Kerry O. Ferris (2007a). Revised and reprinted here with kind permission from Wiley-Blackwell Publishers.

Chapter 2 is based on the article "Through a Glass, Darkly: The Dynamics of Fan–Celebrity Encounters." *Symbolic Interaction* 24(1):25–47, by Kerry O. Ferris (2001). Revised and reprinted here with kind permission from University of California Press.

Chapter 3 is based on the article "Seeing and Being Seen: The Moral Order of Celebrity Sightings." *Journal of Contemporary Ethnography* 33(3):236–264, by Kerry O. Ferris (2004). Revised and reprinted here with kind permission from Sage Publications.

Chapter 4 is based on the article "Ain't Nothing Like the Real Thing, Baby: Celebrity Impersonators and Their Audiences." *Text & Performance Quarterly* 30(1):60–80, by Kerry O. Ferris (2007b). Revised and reprinted here with kind permission from Taylor and Francis Group.

Chapter 5 is based on the article "How Does It Feel to Be a Star? Identifying Emotion on the Red Carpet." *Human Studies* 32(3):133–152, by Scott R. Harris and Kerry O. Ferris (2009). Revised and reprinted here with kind permission from Springer Science and Business Media.

Names of all non-celebrity respondents and research participants have been changed for the purpose of preserving confidentiality. Celebrity names remain unchanged.

1

THE SOCIOLOGY OF CELEBRITY

CELEBRITY AND ITS PUBLIC

Celebrity: we can't get enough of it. Just think of all the publications and broadcasts produced for those of us who are interested in the lives of celebrities. While fan magazines have been around since the early days of motion pictures, outlets like *People* magazine and *E!* television now feed a seemingly insatiable desire for celebrity news 24/7, focusing on the minutiae of celebrities' lives, relying on the invasive tactics of paparazzi for photos, and even turning previously ordinary civilians into celebrities by covering "human interest" stories and supporting the rise of reality television.

These magazines and television shows are only growing in popularity. *People* magazine reported a circulation of 3.75 million in 2006, effectively "beat[ing] back its challengers" (Goldsmith 2006), and its website, People.com, drew a record 51.7 million page views on the day after the 2007 Oscars (Hackett 2007), an all-time high. *TV Week* reports 2.6 million viewers for E!'s 2009 premiere of "Kendra," a reality show spin-off of yet another reality show, "The Girls Next Door" (Adalian 2009), and the same number of viewers for the 2009 finale of "Kourtney and Khloe Take Miami," also a reality spin-off (of "Keeping Up with the Kardashians") (Gilbert 2009). Each broadcast won its cable time slot.

Internet sites also feed the ravenous appetite for celebrity news. Gawker.com's "Stalker" site offers real-time information on New York City celebrity sightings (e.g., "Just left the Russian Tea Room—Jude [Law] and Sienna [Miller] in a back corner booth, heavily making out"), and Perezhilton.com represents a new, particularly snarky breed of celebrity gossip outlets, including TMZ.com and WWTDD.com. These sites can almost instantly consolidate and present information that used to take at least a week to appear in traditional gossip magazines. They can also provide more explicit editorial commentary than print magazines can. Celebrities themselves may maintain Facebook or Twitter sites that keep fans updated on their every move. And Internet fan sites in general are an exploding phenomenon, part of a staggering proliferation of online celebrity information, providing an opportunity for fans to find each other and more easily share their love of particular stars.

Somehow, the phenomenon of celebrity has until recently escaped the scrutiny of the very people best equipped to explain it: sociologists. In this book, we attempt to remedy this neglect of a fascinating topic: fame, celebrity, and their sociological importance.

Studying Celebrity

Until very recently, the study of celebrity was widely held in "serious" academic circles to be a marginal pursuit. Fame and celebrity were seen as trivial topics, unimportant to a comprehensive understanding of the social world. Despite voracious public interest in celebrity, sociology stubbornly ignored it. Only in the last 15–20 years has sociology taken seriously the idea that celebrity is worthy of study. This is painfully ironic, since sociologists are the original theorists of inequality, and fame and celebrity are themselves hierarchical systems.[1] The concerns of prominent sociologists such as Max Weber and C. Wright Mills suggested a sociology of fame and celebrity long before any of their fellows took up the gauntlet. Ultimately, though, it was trends in other disciplines such as literature, cultural and media studies and psychology that finally spurred sociologists to begin considering this most ubiquitous of modern status phenomena.

In this book we take for granted the notion that celebrity is an appropriate object of study for sociology. No defense of the topic will be mounted here. Instead we will offer a new perspective on the growing field of the sociology of celebrity—an empirically-grounded and meaning-centered approach to the topic. Contemporary celebrity deserves an approach, or set of approaches in this case, that can address its unique aspects sociologically. In particular, we make use of a combination of interactional approaches drawn from the traditions of microstructuralism, the negotiated order perspective, and discourse analysis.

Sociology on Celebrity

Despite sociology's long disregard of celebrity, there are seeds of interest planted in several classical texts. You may remember Max Weber from an introductory class, or from a sociological theory course. Weber's (1966) concepts of class, status and party, as well as his consideration of personal charisma as a source of power (1968:215), all beg contemporary application to the question of celebrity. Celebrity is the site of a surplus of contemporary society's charisma—by its very nature it involves individuals with special qualities. From the truly gifted actor or athlete to the exquisitely beautiful supermodel to the simply photogenic "celebutante," celebrities are people who are charismatic and appealing, qualities Weber recognizes as being possible sources of power over others (1968:241). This is visible in the presentation of celebrities (especially athletes) as role models (Fraser and Brown 2002; Kellner 2001; Lines 2001) and as figureheads in movements for social change (Meyer and Gamson 1995). While Weber himself did not (and surely could not) foresee today's version of celebrity, he did hold out the prospect that modern capitalism could generate new forms of status, even beyond what he had theorized or anticipated (1966:27). And indeed it has.

Other early theorists who turned their attention to issues such as recognition, success or heroism, also helped lay the groundwork for later considerations of fame and celebrity (Boorstin 1961; Klapp 1949; Mills 1956). For example, C. Wright Mills (1956:71) acknowledges that fame and success often overlap, making celebrity the "American form of public honor." But Mills also recognizes that not all successes are equal, and hence not all types of fame are equal. He identifies a class of what he calls "professional celebrities"—people who are famous just for being famous, and whose mere visibility is the key to their fame. Daniel Boorstin (1961:57), too, identifies celebrities as "people well-know for their well-knownness." If Mills and Boorstin were alive today, they'd be fascinated with people like Paris Hilton and the Kardashian family, and would argue that their high visibility serves to distract an eager public while the more accomplished (but inevitably less attractive) economic, political, and military elites "really run things" (Mills 1956:93). Orin Klapp (1949:53) takes the separation of fame and true merit even further, and is concerned that awarding "great man" or "popular hero" status to those whose accomplishments in areas like sports or entertainment are "trivial" might actually be dangerous.

In different ways, these foundational theorists foreshadowed a sociology of fame by recognizing the reality of charisma-based social influence while also contemplating its instability and transience. And while these tidbits of theoretical insight have lain mostly undisturbed for decades, they serve as grounds both for sociology's long disregard of fame as a suitable topic and for the discipline's approach to the topic once it did enter the arena of subjects appropriate to study. Eventually, these early theoretical seeds grew into an area of study characterized by a certain moralism: when they do study it, scholars tend to treat celebrity with a certain suspicion.

Celebrity as Pathology

One of the most obvious themes in sociological and other social science research on fame and celebrity is that of "celebrity as pathology." Researchers, theorists and social critics tend to proceed from the assumption that fame and celebrity, in all their manifestations, are scandalous, corrupt, or otherwise contemptible; given these assumptions, it should not be surprising that the resulting findings support the idea of celebrity as pathological.

Some of this pathologizing comes in the form of overt criticism; authors disparage the social and cultural systems that create celebrity (Postman 1984), or trash celebrity itself as an empty, valueless concept (Gitlin 1998). Critic Neal Gabler (1999) is among many who (like some of the theorists discussed in the section above) question the connection between contemporary fame and true achievement. According to these theorists, to be a celebrity in contemporary society does not necessarily mean that one possesses more talent, skill, intelligence or other gifts than the average person—it merely means that one has been more successfully packaged, promoted, and thrust upon the hungry masses (Boorstin 1961; Braudy 1986; Lowenthal 1961; Monaco 1978). This air of disapproval extends to other conceptual approaches to fame and celebrity as well.

S. Mark Young and Drew Pinsky (2006) find that celebrities are exceptionally narcissistic people, and numerous other social psychological analyses link celebrity (or interest in celebrity) to unflattering personality traits. The work of Lynn McCutcheon and her associates (Ashe and McCutcheon 2001; Maltby and McCutcheon 2001; McCutcheon 2002; McCutcheon and Maltby 2002; McCutcheon, Lange and Houran 2002) links fans' "celebrity worship" with a host of negative personality traits, such as dependency and "game-playing" in romantic relationships, shyness, loneliness, authoritarianism, and even "Machiavellianism." These and other takes on the topic seem to assume the worst: that celebrity is dangerous and fans and the rest of society are damaged by their contact with it.

Jake Halpern (2007) laments the perilous and costly extremes to which people are willing to go in order to become famous or to know celebrities. Leo Braudy (1986:618) describes our contemporary obsession with celebrity as a kind of compensation for a lack of "personal honor and responsibility." Wendy Kaminer (2005:58) complains that celebrity culture diminishes our uniqueness and "impoverishes [our] imaginations." West (2005) dubs the advent of celebrity politics a threat to democracy. Richard Schickel (1985) warns that celebrity and our obsession with it creates big-name killers like Mark David Chapman and John Hinckley, Jr.

Wow. Celebrity is pretty scary, isn't it?

And yet fans love it—they (and we) desire it, pursue it, consume it, and can't get enough of it. If, as these scholars posit, celebrity is so bad (and so bad for us) why are we so determined to get a piece of it one way or another?

Celebrity as Commodity

Answer: because it's being sold to us—hard—and we're buying. Many scholars also seem to favor the idea of "celebrity as commodity," which is usually contextualized by a broader critique of capitalism that links it with the celebrity-as-pathology argument. In this argument, when citizens give themselves up to the easy pleasures of capitalism (like mass media, consumerism, and celebrity), they are more readily controlled by tyrants (Adorno and Horkheimer 1993; King 1992; Marcuse 1991). So, from the perspective of scholars, fans and consumers have been duped by capitalism into fancying something worthless and unhealthy.

P. David Marshall (1997) contends that the conspicuous commodification of celebrity is just an indication of capitalism's broader power to commodify all persons. Celebrities therefore embody two of the dominant ideologies of contemporary Western culture: individualism and market capitalism, and they serve as signs through which these ideological discourses get passed on to the population. That makes the celebrity powerful both as an example and as a tool of "mass deception" (Marshall 1997:10). Chris Rojek (2001) also argues for celebrity as commodity—in his analysis, celebrities are the perfect products of capitalist markets, offered up as contemporary replacements for both god and monarch. Ellis Cashmore (2006) joins the refrain, presenting evidence for all of the above (celebrity as replacement god, as opiate of the masses, and as carrier of ideology) before rolling it all into an argument about celebrity as commodity. In addition to being the most glittering product of consumer culture, celebrities are its biggest boosters—in Cashmore's view, celebrities both sell and are sold. In this argument, fans and consumers are taken in by the celebrities themselves, as well as by the system within which celebrity commodities are trafficked. It is yet another way in which contemporary scholars tend toward pathologizing views of celebrity, even as fans and consumers of celebrity enthusiastically seek it out. So far, though, only a few researchers have made attempts to understand the experience of celebrity consumption from the demand side. In order to understand fans' perspectives on celebrity, we argue, interaction-based research is necessary.

Celebrity: Interactional Approaches

The bulk of contemporary research on celebrity is not empirically focused on the lived experiences of fans and consumers (or celebrities, for that matter). However, some scholars have begun to address this gap in the literature. In doing so, they do not reject out of hand the idea that there might be something appealing and attractive about celebrity, and instead consider what that appeal might be. Some of the writings in this vein are theoretical, but most are empirically based and meaning oriented, taking an interactional approach to the topic. This, in our opinion, is the key to unlocking what is distinctive about celebrity from a sociological perspective.

What needs to be done in order to approach a fully-developed sociology of celebrity? A focus on meaning, and on interactional practices of meaning making around the topic of celebrity, is needed. An exploratory spirit and a focus on questions of meaning are necessary to reach a more authentic understanding of the nature of celebrity. What does celebrity mean to the people who produce it, consume it, engage with it, and live it? A focus on appreciating the diversity and complexity of the meanings constructed by these participants is the key to studying the phenomenon of celebrity without pathologizing, romanticizing, or oversimplifying it (à la Matza 1969).

Joshua Gamson provides a model for coming to an appreciative grasp of contemporary celebrity culture in his *Claims to Fame* (1994). He avoids the assumption that celebrity culture is debased or shallow by instead asking "what does celebrity mean to fans?" His methodological strategy focuses on the interaction between the celebrity text, its producers, and its readers/consumers, and the meanings that are constructed in those interactions. He seeks the insights of actual audiences and uses this data to ground his conclusions: most audiences recognize the degree to which celebrity is a commercial construct, and this recognition does not seem to interfere much with their ability to enjoy consuming celebrity (Gamson 1994:148). Their understandings of the constructed nature of celebrity-as-product are woven into their meaning-making processes, and become part of what is pleasurable about consuming celebrity (p. 156). Finally, he admits to being just as fascinated by celebrities as anyone else, something other professors might not be willing to confess!

Other meaning-oriented approaches to celebrity accomplish similar goals, as well. For example, Timothy Dugdale (2000) reveals the range of emotions felt by fans toward celebrities, especially when those celebrities encounter difficulty or tragedy in their everyday lives. Benson Fraser and William Brown (2002) use interviews with Elvis fans and impersonators to tease out the ways in which individuals idealize and identify with celebrities. Phillip Vannini (2004) examines the ways in which fans construct and communicate their interpretations of pop star Avril Lavigne. Patricia and Peter Adler (1989) interview high profile college basketball players about their experiences of fame and their interactions with those who see them as celebrities. Each of these works (and there are also others) allows the meaning of celebrity to emerge from immersion in data and a focus on fans' and celebrities' real-world interactional practices. Their meaning-oriented approach is helping to bridge the gap between previous scholars' criticisms of celebrity and audiences' delight in it.

What to Expect

In this book we also use meaning-centered, empirical research in our attempt to map and analyze the phenomena of celebrity and its study from a sociological perspective. In Chapters 2 and 3 we present two studies of celebrity sightings and other moments of fan–celebrity contact that highlight the thrills and risks of these usually fleeting encounters. In Chapter 4 we analyze the excitement generated even by obvious fakes, as celebrity impersonators and their audiences work together to join fantasy and reality in performance settings. In Chapters 5 and 6 we offer two studies of the often mundane thoughts and feelings of celebrities on the red carpet, where the ordinary and the exotic intermingle as celebrities constitute mind and emotions through talk. We address the interactional dynamics of different aspects of celebrity in contemporary society, focusing on the experiences of those who enact and consume celebrity and the (sometimes contradictory) meanings that are part of those experiences. We do this using three different sociological lenses.

Each of these different lenses is based on the interactionist assumption that meaning is not inherent but is constructed through interaction (Blumer 1969).

In our concern with the norms and rules of situations (such as the fan–celebrity encounters in Chapter 2, or the celebrity sightings in Chapter 3), we reflect the sociological tradition of "microstructuralism." In this tradition, cultural norms are built into the context of each inter-actional situation, and the actors' behavior either conforms to or devi-ates from those norms. You will see, as you read these chapters, the ways in which rules and norms structure the behavior of both fans and celeb-rities, as well as the dilemmas they face in adhering to (or violating) those rules and norms in their distinctive face-to-face encounters. For example, should the fans in Chapter 3 obey the norms of celebrity sighting encounters and avoid giving any indication that they have recognized the star in their midst? Or should they go ahead and break the rules and hope that they can come up with a good justification for why they have done so?

But rules and norms aren't always clear-cut—sometimes there are differences of opinion or competing ideas about what the rules for behavior should be in any given situation. In cases like these, our work tends to reflect the "negotiated order" perspective, which takes the posi-tion that norms are not necessarily fixed but are often negotiated inter-actionally as situations emerge and develop. There are elements of this perspective in several chapters, especially Chapter 4, in which celebrity impersonators and audiences engage in an interactional balancing act to preserve the "impersonation frame" and play the "impersonation game." You may see elements of this perspective in Chapters 2 and 3 as well, since it isn't always entirely clear what makes a fan a stalker, or how a "proper" celebrity should act in public.

Finally, we also delve into the "discourse analysis" perspective (largely in Chapters 5 and 6), which allows us to examine interactional claims-making—how people create meaning as they describe situations and experiences in ordinary talk. The way we talk about things is consequen-tial for how we (and others) understand them. We see this happening in Chapters 5 and 6, as celebrities on the red carpet attribute meanings to situations as they describe their supposed thoughts and feelings. The existence and nature of "minds" and "emotions" are frequently discussed and debated by celebrities in red-carpet interviews.

These three lenses are neither mutually exclusive nor exhaustive, but they do represent a distinctive, interaction- and meaning-based approach to sociological research that contributes to an understanding of the lived experiences of fans and celebrities. We use elements of each tradition to link our empirically-grounded studies of fame and celebrity. In doing so, this book directs attention to the meanings of celebrity and fame that are created in face-to-face social interaction, while also unpacking the important sociological concepts that dwell within those meanings.

2

THE DYNAMICS OF
FAN–CELEBRITY ENCOUNTERS

Who is your favorite celebrity? Why? What makes that celebrity special to you? And how do you know the things you know about him or her? Celebrities are an unavoidable part of everyday life in the 21st century. We are exposed to a seemingly endless stream of news about their lives, loves, good deeds, and bad behavior. Indeed, we may come to feel that we know these celebrities in a certain way, simply because of this onslaught of personal information. So, if we can know celebrities in this way, what kinds of relationships can we have with them? Our relationships with celebrities are idiosyncratic—they mirror but are not perfect copies of our other relationships. They are full of complex motivations, conflicts and rewards, and they are relationships in which some fans may be tempted to go to extremes.

Often, what fans wish for most is the opportunity to pursue these relationships beyond their consumption of celebrity news and into the real world—to "touch greatness" (O'Guinn 1991), so to speak. The fan–celebrity encounter is an interactional moment that highlights the idiosyncrasies of media fanship in the age of film, television and internet. For fans who actively seek out such moments, these encounters are especially significant. Face-to-face encounters are seen as superior to media consumption because they allow fans to expand their knowledge of the actor and to amend some of the asymmetries typical of fan–celebrity relations.

This chapter examines the activities through which certain fans pursue face-to-face encounters and interactions with the celebrities they admire. First we identify some of the strategies these fans use to build relationships and make contact with their favorite actors; the resources and ruses they rely on as they attempt to establish personal contact. We also explore a distinctive tension that such efforts give rise to: fans soon come to recognize that what they think of as acts of devotion may be seen by others, including the celebrities, as strange, obsessive, invasive, and threatening. Fans simultaneously recognize and deny the interpretation of their overtures as threatening and work to differentiate themselves from those who pose a danger to the actors they love. Finally, we examine fans' attempts to show that they are not the stalkers celebrities fear. But first, a bit of background on the world of fans, celebrities, actors, characters, and their relationships with each other.

Background

Active fans of film, television and other media build routines, relationships, and social worlds around their collective activities. In this sense participation in media "fandom" differs little from other group hobbies or extracurricular activities (Stebbins 1980). Yet a unique aspect of media fandom is its focus on imaginary worlds peopled by fictional characters played by professional actors. This means that fans form different sorts of relationships with the objects of their interests than do other hobbyists such as bowlers or gardeners. What is the quality of this difference? Fans' interests lie in both real and fictional incarnations: the people on the television, film, and other screens embody both character and actor identities, and fans come to know the people on these screens despite the fact that they have both real and fictional personae.

How Do Fans "Know" Celebrities?

Horton and Wohl (1956) were among the first researchers to consider the intimacy of electronic media and the possibilities of interactions between audience and performer. They noted that the "illusion of intimacy" provided by television (and other types of electronic media) creates a situation in which the performer and the observer can simulate normal social relations and in which the observer can come to know the performer—if only in a limited way. Since the beginning of media of any sort, there have been fans of individuals whose thoughts, words, and images those media transmit. Braudy's (1986) analysis of fame suggests that fanship is a necessary outgrowth of the dissemination of ideas and images through media: there would be no fame if there were no fans, and there would be no fans if there were no media, whether print or electronic.

Indeed, contemporary developments in electronic media make it ever easier to glean the information that fans crave, and that may help develop fan–celebrity relationships even further: outlets such as Facebook and Twitter provide fans with frequent, tantalizing information updates on their favorite stars, without having to wait for the delivery of a weekly magazine or even a nightly entertainment news show. No matter how they gather their information, fans differ from ordinary consumers of fame because they form especially strong emotional attachments to the objects of their interest, and they can use those attachments as the stepping-stone both to relationships with other fans and to relationships with the famous themselves.

Developing Fan–Celebrity Relationships in the Real World

As fans indulge in and develop their interest in the fictional worlds of media texts, they may also engage in strategies to penetrate the membrane of fame that surrounds their favorite actors and learn what is "real" about the stars themselves. To do this, certain television fans, in particular, engage in another set of activities that are intended to bring them into direct contact with one or more of the actors who play characters in their favorite shows. Direct contact provides something closer to an authentic interactional encounter than does merely viewing an actor portraying a character on-screen, and fans find pleasure and satisfaction in such encounters.

However, in the popular imagination, fans who pursue direct contact with media stars are seen as suspect, possibly unbalanced, and threatening in a variety of ways. Media fans suffer from a tainted reputation because of the violent celebrity stalker, an archetype that has received considerable press in the last two decades.[1] Some media fans, few of whom would consider themselves stalkers, engage in practices designed to bring them into close personal contact with the celebrities they admire. They challenge the boundaries separating reality from fantasy, audience from performer, fame from mundanity, and fan from celebrity. And for better or for worse, the specter of stalking creates the frame within which these fans try to establish personal contact with celebrities. In particular, fans of serial television who engage in such activities attempt to differentiate their own pursuits from those of dangerous stalkers. We turn our attention to these pursuits here.

As noted earlier, fan—celebrity relationships, and the encounters that they engender, are unique sorts of social relations. One distinction between fan—celebrity relationships and "ordinary" social relationships involves the element of *trophy seeking*: fans seek to take away a souvenir of sorts from their encounters with stars. At best, they acquire an autograph or a photograph; at worst, a story about the encounter. In any case, fans seek and display souvenirs from their encounters with celebrities in ways that ordinary social actors in ordinary public place encounters do not. Another distinctive aspect of this type of encounter concerns the fundamental asymmetry of knowledge between the participants: the fan knows far more about the identity of the celebrity than vice versa. These encounters contain asymmetries of power as well—usually favoring the star rather than the fan. These distinctive interactional practices are in addition to the management of the specter of stalking. This chapter examines the social organization of these distinctive interactional encounters, in the interest of exploring how celebrities are known by fans, and what strategies fans may use to pursue that knowledge further.

Data and Methods

The sources of data for this chapter are diverse. The bulk of the data are from a participant observation and interview research project involving groups of active "Star Trek" and soap opera fans. Because of their level of devotion to the shows, and the degree to which their fan activities permeate the rest of their social networks and social worlds, the fans who participated in this project were exceptional. Not all fans are active fans in this sense. But their activities, however exceptional, are versions of more common pursuits and as such are instructive in understanding fan–celebrity relations at many levels.

Participant observation fieldwork and interviews produced revealing data about the meanings of these activities for the fans themselves. As a participant observer over a two-year period, the researcher (Ferris) attended and recorded field notes on a variety of different types of events such as conventions, autograph signings, and personal appearances at store openings at which "Star Trek" and soap opera fans can engage in face-to-face interaction with celebrities. In a series of 20 in-depth interviews with 15 women and five men, she collected fans' accounts of these and other types of celebrity encounters, including chance sightings and the more deliberate hunting expeditions in which some fans engage. Respondents were asked to describe the ways, if any, that they had experienced or sought out contact with their favorite celebrities, including but not limited to writing fan letters, experiencing chance encounters, visiting celebrity workplaces or hangouts, and attending organized personal appearance events. Fans who had engaged in these activities recounted in their own words the details of these encounters as part of telling the larger story of their fanship. The interviews averaged approximately 90 minutes and were taped and transcribed for analysis.[2]

Additional data for this project was collected from Internet fan groups and web sites. Ferris reviewed a wide range of "celebrity journalism" products to become familiar with the types of information about celebrities accessible to fans. She also collected journalistic accounts of celebrity stalkings. These accounts allowed some access to information on cases far more extreme than those of the fans she interviewed, and some also provided information from the celebrity victim's point of view (i.e., some of the newspaper accounts were tales told by celebrity stalking *victims*, not by the *stalkers*). This multifaceted approach produced a broad range of data and a useful diversity of perspectives on the ways fans attempt to and successfully make contact with celebrities.

Familiarity, Knowledge, and Desire

How do fans come to feel that celebrities are people they "know"? The format of what we watch is a factor that contributes to this sense of knowledge and familiarity. Bielby and Harrington (1993), for example, implicate the use of close-ups in the taping of soap operas, since these types of shots simulate the physical closeness of face-to-face conversation. Viewers also have intimate access to the inner lives of the characters, since extremely emotional scenes are soap opera staples. Similarly, Rosen (1986) notes that soap opera worlds provide a sort of surrogate community life for the viewer, as he/she is treated by producers as an all-seeing, all-knowing member of the neighborhood in which his/her favorite characters live. In the case of the sci-fi adventure series "Star Trek," watching the crew of the USS *Enterprise* navigate life-and-death situations weekly (or daily, depending on the local rerun schedule) bonds viewers to crew members as well (see Bacon-Smith 1992; Jenkins 1992).

Viewers thus acquire a deep knowledge of aspects of the shows, including the characters and the actors who play them. This active fan of "All My Children" expresses the depth of her knowledge:

> I kind of have an idea about how Jackson's mind is working and how Erica's mind works . . . when the writers put in something that you know is completely out of character, someone you've been watching for years, and you kind of know what they're thinking and what they're going to do . . . [she shakes her head sorrowfully].

This fan is so familiar with these people, their motivations and actions, that she sometimes has the sense that they have been *misdirected* by writers and producers. This is an indication that she feels she knows the characters better than those who created them.

As fans accumulate knowledge about the characters, they must inevitably approach the distinction between the characters they love and the actors who play those characters, and they may also come to desire first-hand knowledge about, and even contact with, the actors themselves. Here a fan recounts the lunchtime visit to her college dining-hall where James Kiberd of "All My Children" made a public appearance:

I saw him across five feet away from me. He turned around and I waved at him. Not knowing what to say, I had never met anyone famous in my life. He smiled and walked over to me and shook my hand, the holding-on kind. He asked me how I was doing. I said I wanted to hang around, but I had class. He said sorry and he gave me a hug. He was really nice . . . he didn't seem fake at all. He made you feel like he knew you and you were special. I don't think many stars really do that. They say things to act like they appreciate you as a fan, but I don't think they act like your friend.

This account is rich with the sorts of desires and fears that fans have about what their favorite star is really like. The actor's warmth and friendliness, and the apparent sincerity of both, delighted the fan. Even though Kiberd is "on the job" at this public appearance, the fan pronounces their encounter as not "fake": it is Kiberd whom she feels that she has met, not his character, and not an insincere actor wearing an inauthentic public mask.

The attachments formed between viewers and characters in the television-viewing relationship fuel fans' desire to know more about and make contact with celebrities. Much of the work fans do to "get to know" a celebrity is confined to the voracious reading of magazines, to viewing of entertainment-related television shows, and to other types of media consumption designed to increase the fan's wealth of knowledge about the preferences, proclivities, and personal lives of the actors. But fans enjoy the prospect of experiencing face-to-face encounters with their favorite actors, and may in fact go to great lengths to do so.

Fan–Celebrity Encounters

Fans and celebrities may encounter each other in a variety of different settings and circumstances and with varying degrees of intent and mutuality. In many (if not most) fan–celebrity encounters, the fans seek out the celebrities; the celebrities do not seek out the fans. In this section of the chapter, we examine the *pre-staged* and *unstaged* forms of fan–celebrity encounters, and then look at the ways in which fans actively pursue celebrities outside of these types of encounters. In pre-staged encounters, fans buy tickets and stand in line for opportunities to speak with the celebrities they admire; whereas unstaged encounters are chance "sightings" (examined in greater depth in Chapter 3). In the former case, the celebrities are working and hence deliberately courting the attentions of their fans; in the latter case, the celebrities go about their daily rounds, perhaps trying to avoid the attentions of fans. In either case, the ways in which fans seek out and notice celebrities certainly differ from the ways that celebrities orient to and take note of fans.

Public Events: The Pre-staged Encounter

One way for fans to come into contact with celebrities is the pre-staged encounter, in which producers or other groups organize circumscribed opportunities for face-to-face encounters (such as conventions, luncheons, personal appearances, book signings, and golf tournaments). At these events, fans can ask questions or request autographs from celebrities, but only within tightly orchestrated limits. At "Star Trek" conventions, for example, fans can interact directly with celebrities but cannot do so at will. Rather, two officially sanctioned forms of fan—celebrity interaction occur at these events: the onstage question-and-answer session and the autograph signing that often follows.

Part of the now-institutionalized format of every "Star Trek" convention involves onstage appearances by "Star Trek" actors, in which they may give a brief talk, tell a few stories, and then take questions from audience members who have lined up eagerly behind a microphone controlled by a convention staff person. Staff allow each fan one question or comment. Interestingly, both fans and celebrities speak through the amplified convention sound system, but the actor is spotlighted on the stage while the line of fans remains on the less well-lit floor of the auditorium. That is, the fans can see and hear the actor, but the actor can hear, but sometimes not really see, the fans with whom s/he interacts.

Often, fans use their allotted question to mine information about the actor's life outside of her work as a "Star Trek" character. Here, "Star

Trek: Voyager" actor Kate Mulgrew (who plays Captain Janeway) fields a question from a fan in the audience at a "Star Trek" convention:

> The last question was, "Do you ever take your character home with you?" To which Mulgrew replied, "You mean, do I ever walk into the kitchen and say 'Red Alert, you little squirts!'? I try not to, but I do think that to a certain extent Janeway incorporates parts of me as well, and for that reason I do take her home with me."

This exchange, like many others, reveals the fan's interest in gathering information about the actor's personal life, as well as comparing the "real" actor with the character she plays. Mulgrew places herself in her kitchen with her children and then draws a parallel between this personal setting and her familiar professional role on the bridge of the *Voyager*, which allows fans to feel like they know something more about her as a result of this encounter.

Fans may also queue up for the privilege of getting an autograph from their favorite actor. "Star Trek" and soap opera fans will wait in line for hours to have the opportunity for face-to-face interaction with their favorite actor and to come away with tangible proof of that encounter. These, in fact, are the key advantages of the autograph-signing encounter: physical proximity combined with a bit of interactional mutuality, as well as the material artifacts or "trophies" that fans can take away from the encounter. Despite the advantages, though, the regulation of these encounters resembles that of the staged "Q&A" sessions: event staff and security personnel are present at all times:

> The woman who played Saavik [an alien character in a "Star Trek" movie] and one of the show's writers are at autograph tables. There are more people waiting for "Saavik" than for the writer. . . . [T]hey all wait with lit-up faces, clutching photographs up against their chests. They approach the tables one at a time, as directed by the security guard. They hand her the picture, smile broadly, and say things like "You were great" or just "Thanks." Then they walk away and sometimes compare notes with their friends: "She personalized mine!"

Thus a fan may feel that she has received a bit of personal attention from an actor during an autograph encounter; however, she has done so only under the watchful eye of security personnel—an unusual type of interaction, in which the power relations between the interactants are clearly unequal and, therefore, protect the actor while constraining the fan.

The autographed picture is the standard trophy that fans take from these encounters. Some fans, however, manage to have their own photographs taken with the celebrity. This fan snapped a picture of herself with "All My Children" actor John Callahan at a store-opening promotional appearance and gave this account of the encounter:

> I ask, "Can we get a photo with you?" and he replies, "Sure. Ummmm . . ." And I said, "On the side here?" The counter was high, and I didn't want an "over the table" picture. I wanted to go on the side of the counter so I could put my arm around him. So he says, "I'll tell you what we'll do. The best way is to come here," and he points to the side of the counter. "Then you go there. OK, who's gonna shoot it? Hurry. Ready. 1–2–3. Got it . . . OK, thank you guys," and he shakes our hands and it's "See you later."

This account gives a sense of the encounter as both temporally rushed and spatially constrained: there is not much time to take the picture, for the line must be kept moving, and the space is organized to limit physical contact between the actor and his fans. Nonetheless, the fan gets the contact—and the trophy—she wants. In this way she exerts some control over a closely-monitored encounter, even as the actor rushes her through.

Versions of these pre-staged encounters occur at a variety of different officially organized fan-oriented events. Conventions, in-store promotions, charity events, fan club luncheons—each are subject to the oversight of organizers and to the limitations imposed on fan–celebrity contact by the organizers. These tactics create a "scripted" encounter that puts control in the hands of the organizers and celebrities and restricts the actions of the fans. While pre-staged encounters have circumscribed sets of rules regulating the ways in which fans may have contact with celebrities, they do indeed provide contact, and fans are keen to turn that regulated contact into something meaningful for them.

Celebrity Sightings: The Unstaged Encounter

Outside of the constraints of officially organized pre-staged encounters, fans may experience the fortuitous delight of bumping into their favorite actor in the course of their ordinary daily rounds. These, known colloquially as "celebrity-sightings," are "unstaged" encounters. The unstaged encounter can be even more authentic and satisfying than the pre-staged encounter, because it is entirely spontaneous and not engineered in any apparent way by fan, celebrity, or producer.

In chance encounters, the actor does not appear in a professional capacity but merely goes about his daily rounds, as does the fan. Still, the fan may relate to the actor in his character identity, as in this episode, reported in *People* magazine (December 12, 1994):

> [W]hile he was in Los Angeles to promote "Star Trek Generations," [actor Patrick] Stewart found his pockets empty and bravely beamed himself to an ATM in the dead of night. "I knew it was dangerous—the cash machine was in the middle of nowhere," says Stewart, 54. "I was standing in the dark, and the same car circled me twice. I was getting nervous. The machine spat out my cash, and I raced back to my car. But the other car pulled up, turned off its lights, and a huge man got out. 'Captain Picard?' the man yelled. 'Yes,' I said. And the man dropped to his knees and screamed, 'I *love* this town!'"

This fan's reaction to seeing Stewart at the ATM reveals the persistence of the character identity for both fan and actor, and underscores the pleasure he feels at an encounter free from the constraints of a pre-staged event. Simultaneously, however, the actor's reaction acknowledges the fear that freedom from these constraints can engender in stars.

Another Los Angeles "Star Trek" fan recounts a story in which she chanced on "Star Trek" actor Michael Dorn in a local dance club:

> I wanted to say "Hi" to him but it was so loud. . . . [S]o I was like hitting him on the shoulder, and there was just so much mass of humanity. . . . And so I kept banging, and he turned around, and I said "Hi," and he looked at me—oh, he's so cute—and I'm just like melting into a little puddle.

The sight of Dorn in the flesh excites her in part because of its unexpectedness and in part because no competing character persona in this moment subsumes his actor identity. In her understanding of the encounter, he appears as Michael Dorn in an ordinary civilian setting, and the pleasure of the contact almost overwhelms her.

Although satisfying in different ways, both unstaged and pre-staged encounters have their drawbacks. The truly dedicated and desirous fan may chafe at the controls imposed on pre-staged encounters, while unstaged encounters are by nature rare and unreliable. Some fans try to remedy these problems—and gain more power over the situation—by staging their own encounters with celebrities, and they may use creative strategies to do so.

Active Pursuit

Fans who really want to pursue contact with their favorite stars can do so. For example, they may glean information from celebrity journalism and fan-related online media about where they can find celebrities working: studios, on-location assignments, charity events, and the like. With this and other "access information" (Gardner 1988), some fans may try to initiate contact with the actors in the course of their daily rounds. Because most celebrities zealously guard their privacy, these fans may engage in ingenious (and sometimes devious) practices to get this information and to assure such contact.

The Fan-Staged Encounter

Maps of the stars' homes are sold on almost every Hollywood street corner, and their continued popularity indicates that fans have always sought the information necessary to track down celebrities in their private lives. We use the term "fan-staged encounter" to describe the processes through which fans seek out and use access information, effectively hunting down and even interacting with a celebrity in the course of his or her daily rounds. In these fan-staged encounters, fans avoid both the regulations of pre-staged encounters and the unpredictability of unstaged encounters. In fan-staged encounters, the fan is in control.

The relatively public celebrity workplace (television or movie studios or filming locations, theaters, sites of conventions or personal appearances) can serve as the jumping-off point for fans who follow the actors into their private lives, to airports, restaurants, or even their homes. The field note below recounts one fan's tale of her use of the advertised whereabouts of one celebrity to track a whole group of others. This fan made a habit of attending local plays starring members of the "Star Trek" cast, hoping that other cast members would come to see their colleagues' shows. She was often rewarded:

> [Dianne] and some friends saw a play in which several of the "Next Generation" cast members performed. Afterward, they waited for them at the stage door. As they were talking with [their favorite actor], a second actor and the rest of the cast called out from across the parking lot the name of and directions to the restaurant where the cast was dining. Dianne said she and her friends figured, "Why not—they probably won't even notice us," so they used those directions and drove to the restaurant, a tiny Italian place in Hollywood where the "Trek" cast was the only party dining. Dianne says she and her friends were embarrassed but sheepishly stayed and had dinner themselves, never bothering the people at the other table but trying to quiet their excitement at being in the same place.

Dianne and her friends at first used more legitimate means to find the actors at work and then moved on to slightly dodgier practices to dine near them. She used knowledge of a celebrity workplace to gain access to celebrities in the more private, intimate setting of a restaurant and, thus, engineered extended contact with them. Just being in the same restaurant with her favorite actors was exciting for her, and gave her information about their lives that she would not otherwise have possessed.

Soap opera fans, too, can use similar tactics. Following actors from pre-staged events to create a fan-staged encounter involves capitalizing on attendance at official functions to get contact at a more personal level. In the statement below, an "All My Children" fan tells how she persevered in tracking a soap actor after a personal appearance. Despite the actor's reluctance to divulge his travel plans, she managed to see him off at the airport gate (back in the days when it was still possible for non-passengers to do so):

> [At the autograph signing] I said, "American? Or United?" He said, "Yeah, ummmm . . . I don't know." . . . [Later, after the signing] we ran to our car and drove around to the back. We followed the limo to the airport, but instead of going to the terminals, it exited and went into what looked like a parking lot. The sign said "Limos and taxicabs only" but we weren't about to give up yet . . . Went in and looked around . . . and decided to check out American Airlines. We got to the gate and Annie said "There he is!" We looked around, and this time we did see him! . . . He looked up and saw us. Annie just grabbed him and hugged him, and I said I needed a hug. I hugged him quickly and he got on the plane and left.

These fans went to great lengths to have contact with the actor outside of the strictures of the personal appearance situation. But they had to start at that point. They found him "at work" at the personal appearance and followed him to wish him a very personal farewell.

While fans can identify celebrity workplaces with relative ease, they must work harder to find out where a given celebrity lives (Gardner 1988). An underground economy exists that provides celebrity home addresses: with money, luck, some elbow grease, or a bit of each, fans may learn addresses from personal checks, voter and motor vehicle registration information, postal service delivery information, or even purloined studio call sheets (the daily taping schedules that include actors' home addresses so studio limousines can bring them to work). One Los Angeles "Star Trek" fan used her knowledge of the studio location of her favorite show to gather intimate access information about her favorite stars:

> My friend and I snuck onto the [studio] lot—he said he was in some theater group—and we couldn't get onto the set, but I took a bunch of stuff, papers, from the bike messenger's basket when it was parked. I figure that's not stealing, they can just make more Xeroxes. Anyway, the addresses were on it. . . . [T]hey live in the Hills, mostly, and I can go by their houses.

This fan already knew how useful call sheets could be because she once had the opportunity to memorize the addresses of the original "Star Trek" cast from an old call sheet that was among scripts stored at a local university's theater library. She now possesses this access information and may use it to gain further information about the celebrities' life as well.

If knowledge empowers these fans, it also provides pleasure. Joni, a "Trek" fan who works in the travel industry, cherishes the inside information she has because of her job and personal connections.

> Joni tells me that she works for FlyAway and has looked up all the actors' addresses on her computer at work. "They're all frequent flyers," she says. "[One actor] goes up to Lake Tahoe a lot. He has a house up there—my son knows the caretaker. And I know that [another actor] went to Cincinnati and then to Virginia, and I don't think he's come back yet." "Did you ever go by their houses or anything?" I ask. "Oh no," she replies. "I would never use the information. Just to know that I can look at it is enough."

Although she would never use this access information, she has the power to do so. Mostly, however, it is the mere possession of this type of knowledge that is pleasing to Joni.

Knowledge about the comings and goings of favorite celebrities is pleasurable for fans in itself, but it is also valuable because it allows them to stage encounters with celebrities. One "Star Trek" fan who lacked Joni's easy access to information described her strategies for orchestrating an airport rendezvous with her favorite cast member. She kept track of his personal appearance schedule via the fan club newsletter and then, surmising that he would return to Los Angeles on a non-stop flight, called the airlines: "[T]o confirm a reservation on such and such a flight . . . you just give a name and they check it, . . . and if it's on that flight they go, 'Yeah, OK, confirmed.' You just have to know how to ask." She would then meet him at the airport to welcome him back home, planning and conducting the encounter herself.

Finally, one fan cozied up to her favorite soap star's mother at a celebrity golf tournament and offered to send her a copy of the video she was making of the actor's performance in the tournament. Of course, she needed an address to do this:

> I told her I would send her a copy and asked if she was still in the same house. She said she is, but the address has changed. It's changed twice in recent years, and it's such a bother to notify everyone. She proceeded to blurt out her new address for me ([the actor] would die if he knew!). She asked us . . . "Keep it under your hat!" but still!

This fan now possesses a coveted piece of access information and can reach the actor (through his mother) any time she likes.

As is apparent here, fans gather and use access information to make contact with the celebrities they admire. As times change, so do their methods, of course—because of post-9/11 security concerns, there is less access to flight information or airport gates for non-passengers. On the other hand, the website Gawker.com has a "stalker" feature that allows fans to gather information about celebrity habits and whereabouts directly from other fans on the internet, and celebrities themselves may provide such information (perhaps inadvertently) in their Tweets and Facebook updates. This information is critical to organizing and executing fan-staged encounters and is particularly valuable to those fans who engage in active pursuit of celebrities. Fans value this information because it increases their control: they need rely neither on chance nor on the convention schedule but instead are free to contact their favorite celebrities—and pursue their relationships with them—at will.

Fan–Celebrity Encounters and the Specter of Stalking

Once a fan acquires the ability to stage a meeting with a celebrity, the balance of power in the fan–celebrity encounter undergoes a fundamental shift. The security afforded to the celebrity by the scripts and structures of the pre-staged encounters is gone, and the element of chance is removed. As the fan gains knowledge (and hence power), the celebrity loses protection, and the specter of stalking arises. None of the fans in this study would concede that they pose any danger to the actors they pursue. But they make the same creative use of access information that celebrity stalkers do as they seek some way of having independent, regular access to the actors they love, and they may seek a relationship or type of relationship that the actor either does not desire or of which she is unaware. Although the behaviors of certain fans and those of stalkers share some similarities, the fans in this study take care to differentiate themselves from stalkers and the dangers they present. These fans recognize that they must make observable, to the celebrity and to others, the safety and sanity of their own interest, in contrast to the dangerous, unbalanced interest of the obsessed.

These fans claim they pose no threat and that their pursuit of celebrity contact remains acceptably within the range of "normal" relationship behavior, even when others challenge this claim. For example, in the episode in which the "Star Trek" fan follows a group of actors from theater to dinner, she later attempts to normalize the incident in this way: "At a subsequent encounter with one of the actors from that night, he accused her of following them. But she protested, 'We only used the directions [you guys] yelled out!'" In her attempt to frame the directions as freely given rather than illicitly taken, she tries to redefine the encounter as mutual rather than unilateral and, therefore, more like an ordinary, consensual friendship. This is an attempt to distance her behavior from the stalking that it resembles.

This type of claims-making and interpretive work reappears in the case of the stolen studio call sheets. The statement "I figure that's not stealing, they can just make more Xeroxes" is an attempt by the fan to downplay the moral and legal transgression committed in the pursuit of celebrity access information. In the incident at the celebrity golf tournament, another fan exclaims that her favorite soap opera star "would die if he knew" that she had cajoled a home address out of his mother. She recognizes the ill-gotten nature of the information, even as she cherishes it and makes plans to use it.

So, fans can and do recognize that their actions may be seen by others as threatening. Even those who take great pains to get close to celebrities sometimes acknowledge that doing so can make those celebrities uncomfortable. A "Star Trek" fan who works as a security guard at conventions states his opinion about the actors' potential fear of fans:

> The stars? Don't touch 'em, don't approach 'em. . . . When it comes to the stars, most are paranoid and the rest are uneasy. They don't like people jumping out at them. Once I was working the [autograph] line, and this guy jumped out at Quark [a "Star Trek: Deep Space Nine" character played by Armin Shimerman], and he was so upset he cut the signing short.

His comments underscore both the celebrities' awareness of the threats posed by fans and fans' own recognition that celebrities may fear them in this way. Indeed, by working as a convention security guard, this fan gains celebrity contact for himself at the same time that he protects the celebrities from fans just like him.

Fans who acknowledge the possibility that their attentions may frighten the very people they hope to impress may try to account for their actions, to reframe them as non-threatening. Here a group of soap fans who routinely follow their favorite actor all over the state to attend his promotional appearances felt the need to reassure him about their activities.

> One fan exclaimed excitedly: "There's a celebrity golf tournament in Chicago this summer. . . . [W]e're gonna be there." The second fan then said: "[But] then of course you won't be there, right? Don't

be afraid of us!" To which the actor replied: "I'm not afraid of you! I'm, I'm deeply flattered and touched. . . . What's your name?"

Interestingly, in response to the fans' explicit statement that they were non-threatening, the actor responds with his own brand of reassurance—the affirmation that he does not find them frightening but rather understands their attentions as they hope he will, and in fact wants to get to know them better.[3]

Fan-staged encounters yield the celebrity contact fans desire and the control they crave—but may also result in a situation in which they must work to downplay the threat such contact suggests. In a contemporary culture, in which celebrity stalking is a ubiquitous part of the zeitgeist, it seems unavoidable for fans to engage in accounts meant to put celebrities at ease. The problem with such accounts, of course, is that "Don't be afraid of me!" is exactly what a stalker might say, too.

The most famous obsessed fans are well known: Mark Chapman (who obsessed over and killed musician John Lennon), Robert Bardo (who stalked and killed actress Rebecca Shaeffer) and John Hinckley (who attempted to kill President Ronald Reagan to impress actress Jodie Foster, with whom he was obsessed). Because of their association with excess, obsession, and celebrity stalking, fans take pains to differentiate their own pursuits from those of dangerous stalkers.

What is the difference between dangerous and innocuous fan behavior? Clearly, the actions of these fans can be the subject of conflicting interpretation. Their own claims focus on the non-threatening nature of their actions, while others can and do claim that these actions are threatening. A fan may see her attempts to find a celebrity at home as legitimate in the context of furthering their relationship with their favorite star, but those attempts may frighten the actor who has no way of distinguishing a harmless fan from a harmful one. Is she a stalker? She very well may be, but never by her own account.

Conclusion

This chapter has examined some different types of fan–celebrity encounters and the means and strategies by which certain fans pursue knowledge of and personal contact with the celebrities they admire. We have also examined the work these fans do to portray themselves as different from celebrity stalkers, even though they engage in some of the same actions as the dangerous stalkers. Crucial to our understanding of fan–celebrity relations is the notion of "co-presence," or actual face-to-face contact between interactants. This analysis suggests that certain types of relationships can be formed outside of physical co-presence and conventional mutuality; however, it also suggests that, despite this fact, physical co-presence and mutuality are still preferred and sought-after by fans.

Just as the idea of co-presence is crucial to fan–celebrity relations, so is co-presence crucial to Erving Goffman's (1959:15) theories of interaction. This is because co-presence provides for the mutual monitoring of participants in interaction and because co-presence makes it possible to read and react to the verbal and non-verbal expressions of one's co-interactant. While much conventional interaction does occur in situations of co-presence, a growing number of relationships (those facilitated by television, internet and other contemporary electronic media) are conducted via "interactions" conducted almost exclusively outside of co-presence.

Although fans form bonds with celebrities through media consumption, they also seek the mutuality and reciprocity of co-present interactions. Our data highlight the practices by which some fans try to gain that mutuality. Fans take steps to achieve actual contacts and face-to-face interactions with people they know only through mediated contacts and interactions. This makes fan–celebrity contact of even the most circumscribed kind an important bridge between the mediated and the real. A face-to-face encounter with his favorite star allows a fan to feel that he has gathered some evidence about the real person behind the fictional façade, intensifying his relationship with the star.

Fan–celebrity encounters reveal both the pleasure and the perils of radically asymmetrical relations. These encounters feature fundamental imbalances of knowledge (in which the fan can possess a vast storehouse of information about the celebrity, but the celebrity has limited knowledge of the fan) and of power (as control shifts between fan and celebrity, depending on the type of interaction). When these imbalances favor the fan, she has the license to direct the interaction in a way that may fulfill her desires for more knowledge, familiarity and mutuality, but may make the star uneasy. When the celebrity (along with his handlers) has more control, the interaction is generally structured so as to limit fan contact and shield the star from any fan excesses.

How are these ways of knowing one another similar to or different from the ways we know one another in more conventional relationships? The interactional imbalances of fan–celebrity relations distinguish them both from most other types of encounters between the unacquainted and from most "normal" friendships or intimate relations. But it is also true that we experience imbalances of knowledge and power in our "normal" relationships as well. Fans may feel that they are entitled to knowledge of and contact with celebrities (strangers) just as they do with friends, family and colleagues (intimates). But fans and celebrities are "intimate strangers" (Schickel 1985), and that makes all the difference.

While this analysis focuses on an exceptional group of fans, it also points to a more general phenomenon: the ubiquity and importance of media personae in contemporary culture. Even for those who do not pursue contact with celebrities, awareness of their presence is almost unavoidable. Local television news and newspapers, entertainment shows, and a significant portion of the magazines at the local newsstand all focus on the lives of celebrities: even those who protest that they never watch television cannot avoid some knowledge of who is hot and what is popular (Ehrenreich 1990). Television and film characters and actors are part of the everyday lives of even the most casual viewers. For that reason, the fans discussed in this chapter provide instructive case studies of the special relationships between the stars of electronic media and the ordinary people whose devotion fuels the star-making machinery of popular culture.

Analyzing these kinds of fan–celebrity encounters provides a way of examining different types of interaction and investigating relationships that have so far fallen outside the scrutiny of social science. Fans desire and acquire information about, and contact with, celebrities that they hope will remedy the asymmetry of their mediated relation-ships. But as they seek out contact that would seem to mitigate the one-sidedness of those relations, they can overshoot ordinary mutuality and end up fighting off accusations of another type of problematic asymmetry: stalking. Fan–celebrity relations are defined, in the end, by this central irony.

3

SEEING AND BEING SEEN

THE MORAL ORDER OF CELEBRITY SIGHTINGS

Who is the most famous person you have ever met? Where did you meet them? Did you just run into them while you were going about your daily life? If so, you've had a celebrity sighting. And if you've had a celebrity sighting, you've also probably had this dilemma: "What do I do now?" What did you or the other people around you do or say when you were presented with a famous person in your midst? Did you approach the celebrity? Talk to him? Or did you pretend not to notice her at all? How did you feel about your encounter? How did you talk about it to your friends afterward? Believe it or not, these are all questions with sociological ramifications. That is because celebrities are special types of people, and when we encounter them in our ordinary lives, they provide some interesting perspectives on the rules of interaction that guide our everyday encounters but that we normally take for granted. When you run into your neighbor at the supermarket, that's an ordinary encounter, and you know what to do, and you don't have to think about it too hard. But when you run into James Franco or Drew Barrymore at the supermarket, that's an extraordinary encounter, and you don't always know how to react. You do have to think about it, and sometimes it's hard to decide what to do. And that's part of what makes celebrity sightings interesting sociologically.

This chapter examines the intersection of the ordinary and the extraordinary in everyday life by focusing in more detail on celebrity sightings (which we discussed a bit in Chapter 2). Celebrity sightings can happen anywhere—serendipity and surprise are key features of this type of interaction. Celebrity sightings are relatively uncommon and unexpected, and they can happen anywhere, but they tend to occur more frequently in cities such as Los Angeles and New York, where entertainment is a dominant industry and ordinary citizens may see celebrities sitting in a restaurant or in line at a movie theater. Celebrity sightings contrast ordinary and extraordinary frames of meaning and highlight contradictory ways of knowing others, throwing conventional definitions of *stranger* and *intimate* into new, mass-mediated light. And celebrity-sighting narratives—the stories people tell about their encounters—reveal distinctive patterns. These patterns add up to what we'll call a "moral order" of celebrity sightings, as people try to figure out who celebrities are to them (stranger or known other?) and how to respond (ignore them or approach them?).

Celebrity sightings feature a unique tension between stranger (for whom approach is prohibited) and intimate (for whom approach is required). They are also marked by major status differentials as the famous rub elbows with the obscure and the extraordinary and ordinary collide. The presence of a celebrity in an ordinary setting provides an extreme example of what sociologist Erving Goffman (1963) called a "situational impropriety," or something that is out of place in its social setting. In this case, it's the celebrity who is out of place or unexpected, and the ordinary person who has to figure out how to solve the problems this situational impropriety creates by deciding how to respond to the celebrity.

"You'll Never Guess Who I Just Saw!": Celebrity Sightings as Distinctive Encounters

According to Goffman, even the briefest encounters between strangers are governed by a web of rules, rituals, and interactional requirements which, when they are violated, require explanations (or what sociologists sometimes call "accounts"). The etiquette of these encounters is based on certain central rules and norms, such as the basic public courtesy of "civil inattention," which involves looking at someone and then quickly looking away as you approach them on the street, but not giving them any further attention or acknowledging them in any way. But these rules also have a certain fluidity and mutability. Indeed, the rules are suspended in certain situations (for example, public child punishment, in which strangers sometimes intervene; group dog walking, in which strangers amiably interact with one another; and public cellphone usage, in which strangers cannot avoid eavesdropping—all of which involve suspending the rule of civil inattention), and other rules emerge as settings and participants vary (for example, strangers often touch the bellies of pregnant women, stare at the disabled, and conspicuously ignore the homeless, all of which are violations of civil inattention).[1] These examples remind us that there are different types and categories of strangers and that they can therefore interact in different ways when they encounter one another in public places. So, what are the rules and imperatives governing that rare but exhilarating public-place encounter, the celebrity sighting?

Celebrities are technically strangers to their audiences, even as those audience members feel they know the celebrity personally, and react accordingly.[2] Our sense that we know celebrities through mediated contact can create a feeling of entitlement, but their celebrated images are fragile and can be easily shattered, so distinctive interactional rules must be in place for these encounters—a kind of "celebrity etiquette" that differs from the etiquette in place for ordinary encounters.

Celebrity etiquette demands respect for the celebrity's personal space, the violation of which could be perceived as an insult or even an assault. However, because fans feel like they know them, celebrities are also "open" persons and hence cannot guarantee that they will remain unmolested while navigating public space. Approaching someone is usually a privilege of familiarity, while non-familiarity compels non-approach or at the very least respect expressed through what Goffman calls "deference rituals," in which the approached person's status is acknowledged overtly through the greetings and gestures of the approaching person (Goffman 1967:72). These deference rituals preserve the status of those who are deferred to, and their violation threatens it, so, the dilemma of the celebrity sighting is this: which set of interactional rules should be used? Using the wrong set of rules can be risky for both the seer and the celebrity.

Extraordinary versus Ordinary: Competing Frames of Meaning

In addition to the intersection of intimacy and strangeness, celebrity sightings create a tension between ordinary and extraordinary frames of meaning, or ways of interpreting things. This tension produces its own potential conflicts and dilemmas and contributes to the distinctive flavor of these encounters. Each way of interpreting a celebrity sighting has different rules of conduct and deference rituals attached to it, and when they overlap or collide, the everyday actor can find himself in trouble. Both maintaining and changing interpretations requires inter-actional labor, entails interactional risks, and involves the interactional cooperation of others. The appearance of a famous person in an ordinary public setting is usually unexpected, and an ordinary moment becomes extraordinary as a result. When a media figure is encountered in public, this also changes the seer's ordinary way of encountering the celebrity on screen or in a magazine or newspaper photo, and the moment becomes an extraordinary one, requiring different action as well as interpretation.

As fascinating as it is to see a movie star standing, for instance, on a subway platform, it is also problematic for the observer. At one level, we are conditioned to look for and find pleasure in the knowledge that the extraordinary star experiences ordinary things, and celebrity stories are usually constructed to reveal that fame and fortune do not necessarily smooth over the dilemmas of everyday life (Dugdale 2000). But we are also disturbed by the collision of the ideal with the real: when celebrities undergo the mundane ordeals of real life, fans must re-evaluate their idealized image of celebrity life. This is one reason why it may be jarring to see a celebrity standing on the subway platform—they're not supposed to have to do such things, because they are special, aren't they? Intense emotion can be generated in this collision of interpretive frames: excite-ment that the celebrity is there in the first place; disappointment that she doesn't ride in limos like you thought she would; exhilaration at the possibility of interacting with her; fear at the prospect that you might do something wrong; superiority because you're privileged to be in her presence; shame that you aren't more special yourself—all while standing silently on that subway platform, bound by the interactional rules of the setting.

Moral Orders

One of the founding theorists of sociology, Emile Durkheim, suggested that the "moral order" is a shared set of values and norms, prescriptions and proscriptions, punishments and rewards that create and maintain social cohesion, community, and solidarity. Durkheim's notion of the moral order was monolithic, assuming that one set of values and rules applied across the board. Later interpretations of the moral order acknowledge that, just as there are any number of cultures, subcultures, and social settings, so is there a distinctive moral order for each. The specific values and norms of any particular moral order may be very different from those of another—for example, suburbanites tend to stay out of one another's business (Baumgartner 1988) and hence have little conflict, whereas residents of a tiny fishing village are more strenuously involved in each other's lives (Ellis 1986), and because their intimacy is greater, they also have more open conflict. But in all of these cases, the more generic functions of the moral order remain: it facilitates social cohesion, provides a form of social control, offers a set of rules for behavior for which persons are held accountable, and furnishes guidelines for managing conflicts when they arise.

There are countless moral orders that make up the larger social order, and every sector of society has its distinctive moral order. This is especially important to remember in emerging sectors of social life. Despite the obvious differences, we can safely assume that moral expectations and rules for behavior exist in all types of emergent, non-face-to-face relations as well as more traditional interactions. For example, recent research has shown that conflict, competition, and cooperation, as well as social order, social control and social cohesion, are all visible in online communities (Kollock 1999; Reid 1999; Smith 1999). Fan–celebrity relations are a type of interaction that has yet to be comprehensively researched, but there is every reason to presume that celebrity sightings have their own distinctive moral order. This analysis will show that the moral order of celebrity sightings appears informal, spontaneous, and naturally occurring, but it is clearly patterned, and its patterns are visible in participants' stories.

The celebrity sighting creates a distinctive kind of trouble in everyday interaction: How should participants treat this encounter? Continue to treat the encounter within an ordinary interpretive frame? Or to shift out of that frame and into another frame that acknowledges the extraordinary status of the celebrity? To act as if this person is a stranger or an intimate? To abide by the rules or to violate them (with an explanation or justification)? Participants must make on-the-spot calculations and decide how to treat these encounters, and in doing so, seers and celebrities create an emergent moral order, which can then serve as a guide to their actions, either in the moment or in retrospect.

Data and Method

The data for this chapter were gathered in the spring of 2000 by asking a convenience sample of 75 acquaintances, colleagues, and students in Los Angeles to recount in as much detail as possible their most recent celebrity sighting. A celebrity sighting is a serendipitous encounter with any recognizably famous person in the course of ordinary daily rounds (see Ferris 2001). Encounters that involved paid admission or events specifically designed to put celebrities and non-celebrities into contact with one another were excluded, and none of the respondents was involved in occupations that featured routine contact with famous persons. The respondents either wrote down their own accounts or their accounts were recorded in a brief interview and then transcribed for analysis. Some of the accounts were solicited for extra credit in the classroom of a colleague in social psychology. Respondents provided detailed descriptions of the setting, the actions and interactions of others, and their own thoughts, feelings, words, and actions during the encounter. Some respondents provided other artifacts along with their narratives, such as copies of autographs or photos of themselves with the celebrity.

Analysis of these narratives began early in the collection process—in fact, collection of celebrity-sighting stories did not get underway in earnest until after some discernment of patterns had already begun. After noting some of these apparent patterns, stories were solicited and collected in less ephemeral, more easily analyzable forms, as described above. Interview transcripts and written narratives were analyzed using grounded theory methods (Emerson, Fretz, and Shaw 1995; Glaser and Strauss 1967). The textual data were coded to identify themes and patterns in the respondents' accounts. Those themes and patterns were then further specified and developed, with categories and linkages forming the framework for an understanding of the celebrity sighting as a distinctive type of interactional encounter. More focused coding identified the specific rules of conduct attended to by participants in such encounters and pointed toward the larger concept of moral order.

The Interpretive Work of Celebrity-Sighting Encounters

In this chapter, two types of interpretive, interactional work are revealed in seers' narratives of celebrity sightings: *recognition work*, in which seers struggle to define and comprehend the presence of a celebrity in their ordinary world, and *response work*, in which seers present themselves to the celebrity, engineering the encounter to create a particular definition of the situation. As seers accomplish each of these types of interactional work, the moral order of celebrity sightings emerges, and the unwritten rules that govern these encounters and their participants become clear.

Recognition Work

Seers' tales indicate that recognition of a celebrity is not automatic and that the process of recognition is problematic specifically because the presence of the extraordinary challenges routine assumptions about ordinary experience. Seers must work to identify and interpret the meaning of the celebrity's presence in their mundane surroundings, and they do so in a variety of ways.

Double Take

The recognition process may begin only with a sense of *familiarity*: a sense that the person is recognizable in some way, although not always or immediately as a celebrity. In these tales, seers recount their struggles to figure out who it is they are looking at and how they come to recognize these people as known others of some sort.

In this account, for example, the respondent caught the gaze of someone who looked familiar as she sat in a restaurant:

> I went to Jerry's Famous Deli late at night one night with my boyfriend. The place was packed for it being kind of late. Anyway, we were seated and after we had ordered, I looked around the place for want of anything better to do and I caught the glance of a white guy. I just looked away not really looking at him. But something about him seemed familiar, so when I had the chance I looked his way again . . .

While she initially accords the other restaurant patron an ordinary bit of civil inattention, something about this person warrants a second glance. The respondent is unable to verbalize the reason for her double take beyond the fact that "he seemed familiar." But it is that sense of familiarity that compels her to take a second glance and see that the familiar man was comedian Adam Sandler.

Sometimes, there is something about the familiarity that signals celebrity status in particular, even if the celebrity's individual identity is not immediately discernable. In this account, the seer senses that the person is famous, even before she is able to identify him.

> We were at a stoplight. Going in the opposite direction on the other side of the small intersection was [a man] sitting in an old black convertible—I don't know what kind of car it was. I was staring right at him, but I couldn't figure out who he was, although I *knew* he was a celebrity.

Once again, the respondent recognizes the more generic quality of "celebrity" before she grasps the specific identity of the man in the black convertible. In this case, she knew that the feeling of familiarity was the effect of the man's public persona rather than a more reciprocal or personal relationship (in other words, he was not a friend of a friend, or a student in her dance class). Once the recognition of "celebrity" is made, the respondent then had to figure out which celebrity he was (and he was Bruce Willis, as will be discussed below).

There is nothing extraordinary about this type of recognition work per se—in all face-to-face encounters, we may need a few extra moments before we realize who the familiar face is. But in most of our mundane encounters, we do not have to contend with the startling prospect that the familiar face is also a famous one. In these double takes, seers must uproot the ordinary attitude to acknowledge the presence of the extraordinary, something which is often quite difficult (Emerson 1970).

Great Expectations

An additional part of the recognition process that seers cite as confounding is that celebrities often do not look the way we expect them to look. Celebrity-sighting narratives often include the observation that the celebrity is shorter, balder, plainer, more ordinary, or in some other way less spectacular than the respondent may have hoped. These unmet expectations contribute to the recognition conundrum.

Celebrities are not presumed to be ordinary or to appear ordinary, so when they do, seers are surprised. This male respondent who encountered former *Melrose Place* actress Marcia Cross at an outdoor mall noted the following:

> She looked quite plain-Jane and it took me a bit to place her. She looked at me like she knew me and then passed by. She was with ordinary-looking-people friends.

This account reveals the expectation of extraordinariness by noting ordinariness: not only did the actress herself look more ordinary than expected, but her friends did as well. A "plain-Jane" visiting the mall with her "ordinary-looking-people" friends confounds the seer's sense that a media figure should appear extraordinary, as should the people who surround her. It was this ordinariness that made it harder for the respondent to recognize Cross as a celebrity.

This respondent recognized *ER* actress Ming Na's voice in a crowded take-out restaurant before she turned around to see the actress up close:

> It struck me that she sounded exactly the same in person as she did on TV and in the movies. What shocked me was her size. She was teeny tiny, and when I walked by her, I felt that she should be much taller. She left at the same time we did, and we glanced over as she got in a mid-sized family car. I said, "Boring car."

This account does not merely make the observation that Na is short; there is a clear comparison made between expectation and reality. The seer asserts that she already knows what Na should look and sound like, and while the voice meets her expectations, the physical appearance does not. In this respondent's opinion, Na should not only have been taller, but she should also have driven a more glamorous car. These comments reveal that as audience members, we develop expectations that celebrities should be "larger than life," both figuratively and literally, and that these expectations can be dashed when we encounter celebrities in person.

On the other hand, at least one seer indicated that the celebrity she encountered looked exactly as expected. In this case, it was the setting of the encounter that seemed too ordinary:

> I was in Payless Shoe Source. . . . I walked to the counter to pay for my shoes when I saw Camryn Manheim (*The Practice*) walking to the counter with about four or five pairs of black shoes. . . . There was no mistaking her as she looks exactly as she does on TV (twelve earrings and all). However, right away I thought, "What is a celebrity doing in Payless Shoes?" But then I thought, "That's really awesome that a celebrity buys cheap shoes."

Manheim has a formidable physical presence and did not disappoint the seer's expectations in this regard. Instead, the seer fixated on the mundane setting: the celebrity and the respondent are both buying "cheapy shoes," something that ordinary folk do all the time but that television stars are apparently not expected to do. In this moment, in the ordinary setting, the differences between seer and celebrity are minimized.

Great expectations are encouraged by a variety of forces—the aggrandizements of celebrity journalism and elements of hero worship chief among them (Adler and Adler 1989; Dugdale 2000; Klapp 1949). It seems clear that encountering an actual celebrity, especially in an ordinary setting, would present the risk of having these expectations go unmet. However, even if it means that their great expectations are dashed, seers search for and note the ordinary aspects of the extraordinary person in these encounters, as if to rein in the extraordinariness, to make it more manageable in its mundane context.

Proof Positive

When recognition is made, seers confirm the juxtaposition of the ordinary and the extraordinary by searching for some trait or characteristic that they see as authenticating—some piece of evidence that will allow them to present with certainty their celebrity-sighting tale. The clincher is usually some trademark visual or verbal cue that allows the seer to be certain that he is in fact in the presence of a specific celebrity.

In some cases, the celebrity does something that fits easily into the seer's perception of the celebrity's public image. Here, Bruce Willis's hallmark smirk made him identifiable to the woman who saw him while stopped at a traffic light:

> He must have noticed that I was staring at him, 'cause he took off his sunglasses, and stared right back at me. Then I realized that it was Bruce Willis, and he knew that I knew, and he gave me that sly look he always does and nodded his head, then the light turned green and he put his glasses back on.

Willis acted in such a way as to become more identifiable to the seer—he unmasked himself by removing his glasses and then delivered a hallmark facial expression as a sort of confirmation. Indeed, the seer attributes his change in expression to a sense of mutual recognition— she perceives that Willis reacted the way he did because he recognized that he had been recognized. In this way, the narrative injects mutuality into what had been a more asymmetrical episode of gaze work.

Celebrities can reveal identifying attributes to alert seers in apparently unself-conscious ways as well. Here, it was a different action hero's foreign accent that gave him away to this respondent:

> I was on the bike path in Santa Monica when I passed Maria Shriver and Arnold Schwarzenegger . . . towing their son Patrick. The reason I know . . . is because as I passed them Arnold asked [*respondent speaks in a deep voice with an exaggerated Austrian accent*], "Patrick, is dis where you want to stop?"

Schwarzenegger's accent is as recognizable as Willis's grin but is more involuntary and hence subject to different attributions by seers (or in this case, hearers). Schwarzenegger did not produce this utterance to confirm the respondent's recognition of him as a celebrity, but it served this purpose nonetheless.

Recognition of celebrities in public-place encounters is not automatic. Celebrity seers engage in recognition work as they attempt to acknowledge and reconcile the presence of the extraordinary in their ordinary worlds. After an initial double take or moment of disbelief, seers search for both the ordinary features of the celebrity in their midst and the trademark traits that provide proof of the celebrity's extraordinary identity. These features of recognition work reveal expectations about celebrities as being outside the bounds of normalcy in a variety of ways—the way they look, the things they do, the places they go, the cars they drive, the people they associate with—none of these ought to overlap with ordinary "civilian" lifestyles. Confounded by the presence of a star in their mundane world, seers work out a number of different questions in the interactional moment—is that really her or him? How can I be sure? What is she or he doing here? And how should I respond?

Response Work

In response work, the seer himself becomes an actor—or at least a potential actor—in the scenario. In response work, the seer attends to issues that surround the presentation of his ordinary self in the presence of the extraordinary star. How should he react now that he has recognized the celebrity? What are the potential consequences of each possible line of action? In response work, the seer contemplates possibilities and rationales, looking for ways of interfacing with the extraordinary.

Staying Cool

Seers' accounts indicate that the most common post-recognition response is to feign (or fake) non-recognition: to deliberately avoid giving any open indication that the celebrity has been recognized qua celebrity. Feigning non-recognition offers protection against the risks associated with the collision of the extraordinary and the ordinary in the everyday world—it is, as J. Emerson (1970) notes, the easiest course of action to take.[3] Some seers orient to it as a service or gift they provide for the celebrity. Most important, feigning non-recognition sets the standard for ceremonial conduct in celebrity-sighting encounters. This becomes the rule, and exceptions to it must be accounted for.

In this excerpt, the respondent who is waiting for the valet to arrive with her car realizes that she is standing at the curb with a well-known comedian:

> When I looked over, I realized that it was David Spade and two other ladies waiting for their cars. . . . When I first figured out that it was him, I had a difficult time not staring at him and the girls he was with. I tried to play it cool, and not make a big deal of the situation.

The respondent later says that she thinks about Spade's television appearances and remembers favorite performances the entire time she waits for her valet but never approaches Spade, doing her best to pretend that she has not recognized him as a person of special status.

Seers frequently feign non-recognition initially, then comment "post hoc," or afterwards. Seers often tell of making explicit verbal recognition of the sighting only after the celebrity is no longer present or is out of verbal and visual range, as this respondent does:

Once when I was at the airport, Snoop Dogg walked down the hallway towards me with his entourage. I just looked at him, then when he left, I made a remark to my friend with whom I was there . . . but I waited so that it wasn't obvious.

The celebrity is disattended only until the he or she has passed through the immediate setting. Then, special attention can be given, and the frame shifts in a more manageable way. That the recognition of a famous person in public should not be openly noted is an interesting pattern in these data and is an important rule of response work, even when it is violated. Many respondents invoke what they think are important reasons for feigning non-recognition and commenting post hoc:

When I ran into [*General Hospital*'s] Wally Kurth, even though I am a huge fan, I never said anything to him, because I didn't want to bother him. When I told my dad, who was there with me, I told him in a manner that it wouldn't be obvious. . . . I just didn't want to bother him, or disturb him in his personal life.

The celebrity encountered in an ordinary setting is seen by observers as being "in his personal life," and this status somehow creates a social shield for him that is to be breached only under particular circumstances.

Seers make reference to preserving privacy or normalcy for the star as their reason for feigning non-recognition and commenting post hoc. This observer, upon seeing comedian Adam Sandler in a restaurant, notes that all the other patrons are also looking at Sandler without commenting openly. She expresses concern that the celebrity himself must be aware of—and uncomfortable with—the situation:

He was sitting at a small table with just one other male friend. He looked kind of tense, but maybe because he was uncomfortable with the knowledge that hundreds of little eyes were sneaking glances at him and then pretending to ignore him.

Seers' narratives reveal a sense of being charged with preserving celebrities' privacy, even in public places where recognition is clear. Preserving the celebrity's privacy here seems no more than a ruse to this respondent, who feels that everyone involved must be aware of the furtive glances and stifled comments. This is the dilemma and discomfort of recognition for the fan—it is clear to all that Sandler has been recognized and that everyone is "pretending to ignore him." The normalcy of feigned non-recognition is like a gift the seer gives to the celebrity—the gift of ordinariness, an ironic gift, given the obvious familiarity of many of these celebrities.

Preserving the celebrity's privacy is only one part of the moral order here: the seer avoids embarrassment for herself by sticking to these situational rules. This respondent protects both Baby Spice (Emma Lee Bunton) and herself by removing herself from the situation as a friend openly gawks at the celebrity:

> When I was at a tattoo parlor on Sunset, Baby Spice of the Spice Girls showed up with her boyfriend. They were hanging around, and I was there with my two friends, one of whom was saying stuff out loud like, "Isn't that Baby Spice?" So I went outside 'cause I was embarrassed, and didn't want her to think that we recognized her so that she can act like a normal person and not have to worry about her public self.

In their reactions, seers acknowledge that they hold the key to allowing a high-profile public figure to "act like a normal person" in public. Failing to do so can create embarrassment for both the celebrity and the seer because the unspoken rules of the encounter are violated. Said another respondent about her realization that she was standing in line at the Department of Motor Vehicles with *Friends* actor David Schwimmer, "I wanted to jump up and down joyfully and hug and kiss him, but of course I couldn't because he would think I'm some kind of psycho or something."

Celebrities, as the objects of so many asymmetrical, media facilitated relationships with audience members, are vulnerable in public to the recognition and approach of strangers. Among the respondents in this study, the vast consensus seems to be that acknowledging the recognizability of a celebrity in public is to be avoided: "I just took a glance and kept on walking. I hate 'star gawking,'" said one respondent. This particular post-recognition response is central to the moral order of celebrity sightings: seers orient to an imperative that requires them to protect the celebrity from open recognition or risk their own embarrassment (and that of the star) if they do otherwise. In this way, the rule itself is no different from ordinary public-place interactions between strangers—civil inattention requires that we take no special notice of others when we pass them on the street. The problem with celebrity-sighting encounters is that recognition of fame has already complicated the deployment of this particular rule. Special notice has been taken; special status has been detected. Ordinary observers must now try or pretend to ignore these phenomena to reconcile contradictory interactional imperatives.

Your Biggest Fan

Still, some seers do approach celebrities when they recognize them in public. Doing this violates rules of public-place behavior between strangers and leaves the seer vulnerable to judgment, embarrassment, and criticism, and seers' tales reflect this. Therefore, those who approach celebrities in public must offer an account for why they do so, either in the moment or in their retrospective narratives.

The following narrative involves the fan who encountered Camryn Manheim at the shoe store and reveals her concerns about interacting with the actress:

> [Manheim] waited as the cashier rang her up. She was very smiley and appeared friendly so I said to her, "I watch *The Practice*, it's a great show." She smiled very broadly and said, "Thank you. It's great to hear feedback about the show." . . . Overall, she seemed pleasant enough, and I didn't get the feeling she was bothered by my talking to her. I've never actually said anything to a celebrity before, and was a little nervous doing it. I assume they would get

tired of [it]. I also wouldn't want to appear as a star-struck get-a-life fan.

In this account, the fan notes her awareness of the reputational risks associated with talking to a celebrity in public and an orientation to the comfort of the celebrity. Her narrative is constructed to paint Manheim as open to approach—she implies that she would not have spoken to her but for the apparent invitation of "smiley"-ness. She then justifies her interactional gambit after the fact by noting that Manheim "wasn't bothered" by it.

A young woman who encountered movie heart-throb Vince Vaughan at a restaurant happened to have her camera with her and framed her request for a photograph in language that reveals these same concerns:

> I walked up to Vince and said, "Would it be not normal if I took a picture with you now?" He said, "Yeah, sure, no problem." I turned bright red when I realized how idiotic I must have sounded, but at least I got the picture. I said, "Sorry, you are probably really sick of this, but no one would believe me if I told them I met you!"

Again, the fan's concerns are both for her own reputation and for Vaughan's comfort level. Violating the unstated rules of this encounter jeopardizes both, risking the label of "not normal" or even "idiotic," but she's willing to violate these rules (with accompanying justification) to come away from the encounter with proof.

Not every celebrity encountered in public is directly open or vulnerable to approach. Entourages provide buffers of sorts, both for the celebrity and for the seer who wants to approach the celebrity in public. A fan's weight-room encounter with athlete Magic Johnson through his personal trainer illustrates this:

> I asked the trainer working with him if Magic minded if I said "hello." He told me that it would be all right just as long as I didn't ask for his autograph. I completely understood why, and promised that I wouldn't. Magic just kept treading away on the treadmill as

he politely responded. . . . I told him I couldn't leave without saying hello and telling him how much of a fan I am. . . . He shook my hand and asked me to give him a high five!

Here, the trainer gives permission and clarifies the parameters for the encounter, which can then proceed smoothly. The trainer's role as an interactional broker ratifies and legitimizes the encounter and, more important, makes the rules of the encounter explicit, smoothing it over for everyone. The fan can have his moment of contact, within agreed upon limits, and Johnson can continue his workout with minimal disruption. Note that in this account, no mention is made of embarrassment, idiocy, or abnormality, as in so many others. The trainer's facilitation is critical to this apparent increase in all participants' comfort levels.

When a person of special status is encountered in an ordinary public place, deference to that special status is a key feature of the prevailing moral order. In the case of ordinary persons' encounters with celebrities, avoidance rituals prevail—the celebrity's personal space should not be violated, verbally or visually. The person who does so risks his own embarrassment and the aggravation of the celebrity. So, when civilians do approach celebrities in public, their accounts reveal an orientation to a set of unspoken rules about how to do this. They fear loss of face, either by approaching the celebrity in the wrong way or by approaching the celebrity at all.[4] They also fear some violation of the celebrity's "right" to be a private person in public, despite the fact that most of the celebrities encountered by these respondents are widely recognizable and cannot have a reasonable expectation of remaining anonymous in a public setting. Seers' accounts reveal an orientation to a moral order of celebrity sightings, a code of behavior to which they are held accountable.

Two Thumbs Down

When celebrities encounter non-celebrities in public, they are themselves expected to do their part in upholding the moral order of the situation. The final type of response work in celebrity-sighting tales involves the seers' evaluations of the behavior of celebrities as either appropriate or inappropriate to their extraordinary status.

Those who seem too interested in drawing the attention of others are seen in an unsavory light, as in this account of a fan who encounters a high-profile male model at a Hollywood shop:

> Tyson [Beckford] the supermodel showed up. I pretended that he was just another person and didn't pay too much attention to him . . . though I think he wanted the attention 'cause he was loud and showed up in a limo, and was coming and going, in and out with his entourage.

This respondent seemed intent on deliberately withholding attention from Tyson, who by her reckoning was trying too hard to gain it. This punitive orientation indicates that in addition to rules for seers, there are also rules for celebrities when they appear in public. The loudness, the limousine, and the entourage, as well as the repeated entrances and exits, all are taken as evidence by the seer that Tyson wants to be seen. He violates the unspoken arrangement by which seers should at least affect non-recognition, with his antics making it impossible for her to abide by that rule.

On the other hand, celebrities who try too hard to conceal their recognizability are also seen as strange or disagreeable. This respondent encountered actor Alec Baldwin at the supermarket:

> When I was in the checkout line, I noticed a strange man in the next line. Keep in mind that this was in the middle of June. The man was wearing tattered jeans, an old T-shirt, a detective hat (you know), a trench coat, sunglasses, and had lots of stubble beard. Well, I recognized him, and kept looking back over my shoulder to make sure, and it was him, I knew it when I heard him ask the cashier "How much?" Well, in the parking lot he got into a BMW and drove away.

Baldwin, dressed like a pulp-fiction private eye, draws attention because he is too obviously incognito, defeating the purpose of the disguise by increasing the curiosity of passers-by like this respondent.

The disguise invites attention, almost as obviously as a limousine and an entourage, and in fact has lured the seer into making the very recognition the disguise may have been designed to avoid. Once again, the celebrity is now seen as being in violation of the moral order, by manipulating his recognizability. Despite the celebrity's extraordinary status and power in our media-saturated society, when he appears in public places, his fates, metaphoric and literal, are still in the hands of his observers.

Discussion

Major rituals and ceremonial occasions—birthdays, graduations, weddings, parades—are widely recognized as opportunities to affirm, replicate, or even challenge the moral order of a civilization; Goffman urges us to see this moral order (and its affirmations, replications, and challenges) in everyday interactional ritual and ceremony as well. The moral order is performed in every social interaction, common or uncommon, ordinary or extraordinary. The "minor ceremonies" (Goffman 1967:91) of celebrity sightings underscore and reproduce the contemporary secular moral orders of status, fame, and reputation in everyday life. The celebrity sighting is a special kind of public-place encounter, featuring its own codes of behavior for participants and its own principles of moral accountability for both seers and celebrities. Seers' tales of recognition work and response work demonstrate the presence of a moral order in celebrity sightings. This particular moral order revolves around the special status of the celebrity, and the clashing frames of meaning that occur in celebrity-sighting encounters.

Despite the indisputably public face of the contemporary media figure, those who encounter celebrities in public tell of feeling compelled to keep private their recognition of these public figures. Feigning nonrecognition is a service seers perform for celebrities, and by their own accounts, providing this service earns seers a certain virtue or moral integrity. But restraint and empathy must also be demonstrated when the code is broken. Those who do approach celebrities in public try to mitigate this violation in their accounts, expressing awareness of or sympathy for the plight of the public figure. And celebrities who either seem too interested in drawing the attention of onlookers in public or seem to try too hard to conceal their identities in public are the objects of disdain in seers' accounts, as this upsets the delicate balance of recognition and recognizability in these encounters.

The emergent rules of conduct revealed in celebrity-sighting narratives constitute a moral order because they serve to maintain and police various status boundaries: ordinary versus extraordinary, obscurity versus fame, stranger versus intimate. The celebrity sighting is an encounter that endangers these distinctions: the presence of the extraordinary person in the ordinary setting threatens to disorganize the seer's social world. The distinctive moral order of celebrity sightings responds to and helps contain that threat and manages the clashing frames of meaning through ritualized rules of conduct.

When the extraordinary and the ordinary intersect in everyday life, as they do in celebrity sightings, the stakes are high and so are the potential rewards. If the seer behaves herself properly, she comes away with at least an exciting story to tell about her encounter with fame and at most a picture or autograph as a trophy of that encounter. But if the seer fails to behave properly, he may have only the embarrassment of rejection to show for his accidental brush with greatness. The dynamics of celebrity sightings feature a moral order laden with risk and reward, and the accounts of the seers reveal a clear orientation toward reaping rewards while reducing risks.

So, did you see yourself in this analysis? Have you done these same things when you had a celebrity sighting? Have you worried about how to act or whether to approach a celebrity when you encountered him or her in public? What did you decide? How did you react to the famous person in your mundane world? Maybe you've never had a celebrity sighting yourself, but someday you probably will. And now you'll be able to recognize the sociological significance of this type of fan–celebrity encounters. You may even be able to analyze your celebrity sighting while it is happening, evaluating whether you adhere to the moral order of the situation, or whether you violate it. Sociological insight doesn't take the fun out of encounters like these—in fact, it can make them even more interesting.

4

"AIN'T NOTHING LIKE THE REAL THING, BABY"

FRAMING CELEBRITY IMPERSONATOR PERFORMANCES

Christine Goings, the public relations director of a Las Vegas hotel-casino, tells an amusing story about some confusion that arose during the weekend of a big celebrity impersonator conference held a few years ago at the hotel. She received a call from a casino floor supervisor saying that Oprah Winfrey was in the hotel and that she wanted permission to shoot some video. Christine laughed into the telephone: "Oh, no, no, don't worry about it, it's not the real Oprah . . . we've got a celebrity impersonator convention in the hotel, so she's just a fake." The floor supervisor was silent for a moment, and then said cautiously, "No . . . she's the real thing, and she wants to shoot this video now." Christine again laughed and assured the supervisor that this Oprah could not possibly be the real thing. The supervisor again demurred, saying he was quite sure she was real. Back and forth this disagreement went until Christine, exasperated, finally agreed to come down to the floor and shoo away the fake Oprah. She felt irritated that the supervisor could not seem to do this chore himself.

To her surprise, she found herself face to face with the real Winfrey, her entourage and camera crew! She apologized profusely, helped them arrange the filming they needed, and then proceeded to repeat the story to everyone she spoke to for the rest of the day, chuckling over the irony of the real Oprah arriving unannounced in the midst of a hotel full of fake celebrities.

Christine's quarrel with the floor supervisor over what constitutes the "real" Oprah Winfrey illustrates how tricky it can be to distinguish the real from the unreal, especially in a setting that skews toward the latter. Her confidence that she was dealing with an Oprah impersonator arose from the interpretive frame within which she was operating at the time—a frame within which *all* celebrities were fakes and *none* were real, at least for that weekend. This frame guided her interpretation of all her interactions, including the disagreement with the floor supervisor: had his call come in on any other weekend she would undoubtedly have rushed to roll out the red carpet for Ms. Winfrey and her delegation. But the impersonation frame shaped her interactions within the hotel that weekend, and its persistence is a testament to the potential power of the intangible over the tangible, of interpretation over fact, and of fantasy over reality. Within the right interactional frame, almost anything is possible. So what is the difference between reality and fantasy? How do we distinguish one from the other? And what makes a fake celebrity just as good as (or even better than) the real thing?

This chapter explores the interactional framing of celebrity impersonator performances, and conceptualizes impersonation as a collaborative game that takes place within this distinctive interpretive frame. Performer and audience work together to maintain an interactional boundary within which the real and the unreal coexist comfortably. Within this boundary, the impersonator's imitative performance can include references to its own unreality without ruining the audience's experience of "Elvis" or "Cher" or "Britney"; the audience can also respond to those references in ways that make it clear that they both recognize the fakery of the performance and are willing to suspend that recognition while within the impersonation frame. These interactional moves, between performer and audience, across the border between reality and fantasy, constitute the impersonation game, and help create and sustain a pleasurable experience for the audience, even though these celebrities are fake.

Game and Frame in Celebrity Impersonation

Celebrity impersonation involves performer and audience in a collaborative game in which a "successful" performance is a joint effort—not just the task of the performer, but of the audience as well. When they are together in the theater, celebrity impersonators and their audiences mutually orient to the maintenance of a distinctive interpretive frame (Goffman 1974:124) in which everyone knows that it's not the real Elvis (or Madonna or Prince) onstage, but manifestly suspends this observation of fact for the duration of the performance. In most cases, it is possible to make reference to this seemingly contradictory situation without threatening the impersonation frame; in fact, making and responding to these references to out-of-game reality are critical parts of the game. Only in very rare cases is the frame broken or the game spoiled by the open identification of its fakery.

The Impersonation Frame

Erving Goffman (1974) uses the term "frame" to describe the symbolic structures that guide people in their interpretations of interactional situations. A frame shapes what people know about a situation by emphasizing some interpretive possibilities while excluding others— frames help us know what is happening, what the rules are, and how we should respond. Celebrity impersonation occurs within a fairly standard theatrical frame (Goffman 1974:124): performances are staged and scripted, and just about everyone involved is aware of that. But celebrity impersonator performances also involve a level of what Goffman (1974:133) calls "frame sophistication," a kind of cooperative manage-ment of multiple contextual layers in which the artists and audience members simultaneously recognize and agree to overlook the presence of those layers.

In both the theatrical frame and the impersonation frame, what happens onstage is constructed and artificial, and the audience both recognizes and "holds this understanding to one side" (Goffman 1974:136) in order to maintain the quality of mind necessary to absorb the performance. (Whether they will ultimately enjoy it or not is another question entirely.) But only in the impersonation frame do performers project multiple and seemingly contradictory messages about their performance to the audience. That is, sometimes imper-sonators act like they are the real thing, and sometimes they act like they know they are not the real thing. Celebrity impersonators move back and forth between the type of sincere imitation that represents the traditional theatrical frame (in which all in the theater agree that the performer has taken on a role) and the playful improvisation that complicates that traditional frame (in which a performer makes a "wink wink, nudge nudge" reference to his/her role-taking). In the impersonation frame, the outside world (in which the actual celebrity exists or existed) never disappears. In fact, it provides a tantalizing resource for performers and audiences alike.

While impersonators' insinuations that they are not the real thing may momentarily jolt audience illusions, these devices do not necessarily challenge the larger assumptions about stage performance more generally. In other words, when an Elvis impersonator deliberately mentions having visited The King's grave at Graceland, he generates a contradiction to the traditional theatrical assumption that he "is Elvis." In that moment, he becomes a performer in a white sequined jumpsuit who cannot be Elvis, because Elvis is R.I.P. in Tennessee. However, even a reference to the dead Elvis is still part of the distinctive impersonation frame, in which playful asides such as this are integrated into the performance, and humorous intrusions are artfully managed (Goffman 1961:48). Operating within the impersonation frame means juggling multiple personae, contexts, and levels of awareness.

An unintentional glitch may disrupt the "celebrity impersonator as real thing" fantasy, but can usually be managed as part of a traditional theatrical frame where performers' errors are disattended by audiences (Goffman 1974:133). So, celebrity impersonators and their audiences operate in a frame-within-a-frame: the impersonation frame represents an agreement among participants that playful reminders of the performance's unreality are acceptable, and this frame is contained within the more familiar theatrical frame. Celebrity impersonators and their audience members are "collaborators in unreality" (Goffman 1974:136) in ways that are one step more complicated than those of ordinary actors and theatergoers. Celebrity impersonators and their audiences are aware of the constructed nature of their amusements, even while in the process of constructing them.

The Impersonation Game

The term "game" can be used to mean a competitive contest, such as football, poker or chess; it can also describe cons, deceptions or double-crossings of various sorts. But "game" doesn't only describe explicit win-lose situations—Goffman (1961:27) is also willing to use the term to describe just about any kind of rule-governed, multiple-actor "world-building" activity. Games, in this sense, require shared involvement in an encounter, feature a body of rules to which participants are jointly oriented, and occur within specific interactional boundaries. Of the various examples he cites, stage plays are included (Goffman 1961:73), as are war exercises (p. 36), certain occupations such as banking or publishing (p. 37), and even cocktail parties (p. 78). In other words, the concept of the game, and participation in it (play), can be extended to a diverse array of social situations.

The celebrity impersonator performance is a type of game played by audience and performer. It meets Goffman's criteria in that audience members and performers come together in a specific setting, with a shared focus and a set of rules to guide their activities. For example, gaming encounters are often engineered so as to maximize their potential to engross their participants. A celebrity impersonator performance is no exception. Enclosure in a theatrical space with stage, curtains, lightings, props and music all serve to create a setting with specific boundaries designed to "hold participants entranced" (Goffman 1961:67). Also, within the theatrical frame, certain rules apply: the action is onstage, for example, and there is a limited range of acceptable audience responses to that action. Audience and performer are together in a dedicated space with a shared general focus and a set of basic rules to work with—conditions under which a game can begin.

One of the key elements in Goffman's concept of the game is the prospect of fun. Fun is the product of engagement and immersion in the activity, in particular the maintenance of a boundary or "membrane" (Goffman 1961:65) that seals the participants off from other social worlds, concerns, and meanings. Fun in games is the result of main-taining a successful balance between the "entrancements" to be had within the boundary and the "intrusions" from without (p. 73). This does not mean that intrusions must be avoided or prevented, only that they must be skillfully managed when they occur. Indeed, problematic incidents can be integrated into the game's world of meaning (p. 48) using tact, charm and other sorts of acumen; and the risks posed by these intrusions can actually be part of a successful (and fun) game. This is especially true within the impersonation frame, since sardonic asides that might otherwise function as intrusive observations of the unreality and absurdity of the whole enterprise instead become part of the fun.

Research Scene, Methods and Data

Because celebrity impersonation is an area of social life you might not be familiar with, a bit of background on the scene is in order, in addition to a more conventional discussion of methodology.

The Celebrity Impersonation Scene

Celebrity impersonators perform in a variety of venues, from birthday parties to Las Vegas revues to cruise ships to television commercials. Former Iraqi president Saddam Hussein had several impersonators who attended events in his name, essentially serving as decoys for potential assassins (Stewart 2003). Obviously, different settings and types of performance require different attributes: "dead ringers" (perfect look-alikes) for still photography, sound- and move-alikes for live singing and dancing (where costuming and makeup can hide visual disparities), affability for handing out freebies at trade shows (where thousands of attendees hurry by for a handshake), and even defensive weapons skills (for those faux Saddams). On the 2007 ABC reality show, "The Next Best Thing," celebrity impersonators competed in an "American Idol" type elimination contest to determine who had the best "total package": voice, looks, and mannerisms.

There are a number of talent agents and agencies that specialize in celebrity impersonators, but an unknown number of impersonators are represented by non-specialists, or not represented at all. At least three of the bigger celebrity impersonator agencies—California-based International Celebrity Images (ICI), Georgia-based International Guild for Impersonators and Tribute Artists (IGCITA), and California-based

Celebrity Impersonators—host conventions for impersonators (though IGCITA folded in 2006); ICI also organizes the annual "Reel Awards," and a Florida convention group hosts the "Cloneys," both a kind of celebrity impersonator Oscars. These events seem largely designed to generate publicity, recruit performers to agencies, and provide networking opportunities.

A celebrity impersonator's draw fluctuates with the fortunes of those s/he impersonates, with pay rates and demand changing as the real celebrity's popularity, reputation and status change. For example, the late Michael Jackson, whose unsavory personal and legal troubles, as well as his untimely death, might seem to hinder the career prospects of his impersonators. When the real Jackson endured a career-damaging child molestation trial, Jackson impersonators and their agents feared the chilling effect of bad publicity on their bookings (Robinson 2004). However, even during the trial, some Jackson impersonators saw an uptick in interest in their services. Daily trial re-enactments ran on *E! Entertainment Television*, with impersonator Edward Moss in the defendant's seat. Jokes and skits about Jackson continue to proliferate on late night television even after his death, and both spoof photo shoots in magazines such as *GQ* (Friedman and Buck 2006:4311) and heartfelt tributes (Huppke 2009) have kept impersonators of even the dead and disgraced in business.

Statistics on celebrity impersonators' earnings are difficult to come by, as there is no single overarching professional association or union that represents all impersonators. In a 2001 article, the *Los Angeles Business Journal* reported hourly rates charged by celebrity impersonators that ranged from $250 an hour for a Groucho Marx impersonator to $3000 an hour for a Bill Clinton impersonator (Greenberg 2001). But celebrity impersonators, like other types of performers, generally do not work standard 40-hour weeks. One agent's estimate (Jeff J., 5/29/06, personal communication) is that only 15–20 percent of celebrity impersonators make a living working full time as impersonators. Others maintain "day jobs" that may or may not be entertainment-related. Finally, fees vary based on character, experience, location and type of booking. So, it is difficult to estimate how much money is made and spent on celebrity impersonator services in a year. Given the proliferation of impersonator shows in towns across America (not just glitzy resort venues like Las Vegas or Atlantic City, but places like Detroit, Provo and Baton Rouge) and the countless daily appearances of impersonators at conventions, trade shows, corporate meetings, grand openings, fund raisers, political rallies and bachelor parties, celebrity impersonators appear entitled to claim a small but significant slice of the entertainment industry pie.

Data and Methods

Much of the data for this chapter were gathered at three consecutive meetings of the Convention of Celebrity Impersonators, held annually in Las Vegas. The CCI is a 4-day gathering of professional celebrity impersonators from across the country, along with agents, managers, industry booking reps, and a small cluster of reporters, photographers, and documentarians. The CCI is much like an ordinary professional association conference: there are the usual luncheons and panel sessions in windowless hotel meeting rooms. At CCI, however, all the attendees are in costume. Evenings involve performing in talent showcases, attending other Las Vegas impersonator shows and, starting in 2007, attending the Reel Awards, which are now scheduled during the CCI. These data gathering trips involved sitting in on all panel sessions, attending the luncheons, dinners and performances, and doing informal interviews with impersonators (15), agents (2), and other attendees (one spouse of an impersonator, and three members of the organizing staff). In addition to the three 4-day fieldwork trips for CCI meetings, there were four additional 3-day fieldwork trips to Las Vegas and one 3-day fieldwork trip to Branson, Missouri, at other times of year, where observations and interviews were conducted with non-CCI-affiliated performers.

Formal, open-ended interviews were conducted with 17 professional celebrity impersonators in Las Vegas (14), Illinois (2), and New York (1). Of the Las Vegas impersonators interviewed, half were onstage performers and half were dealer-performers (described below). One of the Illinois impersonators was an onstage performer with a different performance-oriented "day job," and the other, along with the New York impersonator, was an onstage performer who had appeared on a national television show about celebrity impersonators. All observations were recorded in the form of written fieldnotes, while interviews were recorded and transcribed. Photographs and videos of performers, their performances, and their interactions with audiences are also part of this data set. Other parts of the data set include video clips from television broadcasts, and newspaper and magazine clippings on topics related to impersonation. Grounded theory methods were used to identify and develop themes and patterns in the data (Emerson, Fretz, and Shaw 1995; Glaser and Strauss 1967).

Framing the Impersonation Game

Impersonator performances invoke the personae of the real artists being impersonated, as well as providing the audience with all sorts of cues and clues that what they are seeing is not the real thing. Setting the stage for this type of performance involves familiar elements of ordinary theatrical framing, as well as impersonation-specific elements that highlight what is unique about these particular performances. For example, at the beginning of a "Stars on Parade" performance, the lights go down and the audience quiets and turns its attention to the stage. Within standard theatrical space such as that used by "Stars," seating arrangements, staging conventions and lighting maneuvers all combine to signal to the audience what is about to occur (a show on the stage) and how they ought to respond (attentively). These are traditional elements of theatrical framing, present in most theatre performances, and are crucial to creating an absorbing setting for performer and audience for the duration of the show. This type of stage-setting is both familiar and necessary as part of the theatrical frame.

But at "Stars" impersonator shows, before the curtains open or any performers appear, an announcement booms out over the public address system into the darkened theater:

> "Welcome to 'Stars on Parade,' an unbelievable live recreation
> of your favorite artists and music. Each Stars performer uses

their own natural voice and plays their own instruments—no lip-synching!"

This announcement is a jumble of references to both authenticity and the lack thereof. The announcer promises a performance that is "unbelievable" and a "recreation" at the same time as it is "live" and "natural." These mixed messages about reality and fantasy provide a preview of the distinctive impersonation frame that will come to shape the interactions between audience and performer throughout the show.

Frames serve as interpretive resources for interactants, and so deliberate framing devices such as stage sets are intended to direct the interpretations of audiences. At "Stars," impersonators perform on stages flanked by huge banks of video screens. Seven screens on each side play video montages while the celebrity impersonator performs. These montages depict the real artist, using silent music videos, footage of past performances, still photos and album cover art, and in almost every case, also include footage of real audiences responding to the real artist. So, if a Tom Jones impersonator is performing onstage, video of the real Jones is projected on 14 video screens surrounding the stage, as if to remind the audience that the man onstage is emulating the man on screen, and to invite comparison. In addition, when shots of the real Jones' real audience (throngs of frenzied women notorious for throwing panties at the stage) are also projected on the screens, the audience is invited to do some emulating themselves. This audience imagery suggests how the current audience might respond to the impersonator, and is especially powerful in cases where the real audiences were (or are) as legendary as the real performers themselves, as in the case of Beatlemaniacs, Elvis Presley fans or Jimmy Buffett's "Parrot Heads."

In cases like these, the distinctions between audience and performer are blurred, as audiences respond to onstage performances with performances of their own. Fans scream at, sing along with, and beckon to faux Beatles, Elvises, Tom Joneses, and Jimmy Buffets in impersonation of the real performers' fans. A kind of "Rocky Horror Picture Show" phenomenon can occur at impersonator performances, but instead of dressing up as Brad, Janet or Frank N. Furter and throwing toast at the screen, the fans merely masquerade as a version of themselves. The audience apes another audience while the performer impersonates another performer.

Using video imagery to set the stage is not a strategy exclusive to celebrity impersonator performances, but the particular images used at "Stars" strongly suggest that the interactional frame for these performances is different from that of a regular play or concert. Both the image on the screen and the performer on the stage are simulations; in the absence of a real Tom Jones, only these versions are available to the audience. Yet both are also real in different senses: the flesh-and-blood performer onstage is certainly real (as the pre-show announcement reminds us), if not the real Jones, while the image on the video monitor is of the real Jones, not the impersonator. Juxtaposing different ways of being real with different ways of being an imitation introduces the impersonation frame as a special kind of boundary around a distinctive type of performance. It also sets the stage for an impersonation game in which interactants can play by rules that are different from those in the ordinary world or in most performance contexts.

Playing the Game

Sustaining the celebrity impersonation frame involves what some impersonators call "playing the game." By this, they mean an active collaboration with audience members to maintain the fantasy that the impersonator is "the real thing"—all the while knowing that s/he's not. Impersonation, like any performance, requires collaboration between audience and performer within the theatrical frame. Impersonation is a special case, however, because the audience's part in the collaboration requires both attending to and disattending the fact that the impersonator is acting in the role of someone who is real and well-known, but who is not present (and who may even be dead).

So, how is this game actually played? What are the interactional moves made by performers and audience members that support the sense that they are engaged in play? What gets said and done within the impersonation frame that constructs an engrossing world within which serious authenticity and sly send-ups can coexist?

The celebrity impersonation game involves deceiving and being deceived while simultaneously recognizing and holding aside the recognition that no one is really deceived. In explicit acknowledgment of the cooperation that is required to sustain this type of play, a Jay Leno impersonator notes audiences' eagerness to "be fooled." He includes himself in those ranks: even though he's in the business of fooling, he's not too jaded or above the impulse to be taken in himself:

> People want to be fooled. I remember years and years and years ago I was at a bar up on the East Coast and there was a guy there who looked a dead ringer to Burt Reynolds. Well, I felt like I was with Burt Reynolds. He was doing the whole bit standing around [in Burt Reynolds voice] "Hey, how you doing?" I want to be fooled. And people love being fooled. They want to feel like, you know, most people aren't going to meet Jay Leno or Elvis or whoever. And they will suspend their disbelief long enough to have fun . . .

He realizes that audiences recognize the difference between the celebrity impersonator and the real thing, but that they are willing to temporarily shelve that recognition while they watch the impersonation, for the sake of "fun." He also suggests that part of the enjoyment of watching an impersonator perform involves actively playing along with the celebrity impersonation game in winking solidarity with its other participants.

One of the strategies used by performers to play the impersonation game involves the use of grammatical gymnastics onstage that allow them to remain in-character while still reminding onlookers that they are not, in fact, the real thing. For example, an impersonator herself never says "I am Aretha Franklin (or Prince, or Elvis)" or anything else that explicitly makes such a claim. When she does speak in the first person, an impersonator generally says something non-committal (like "This is one of my favorites!" "Wanna see me dance?" or "Does my hair look OK?") that could just as easily be said by the real Aretha, Prince, or Elvis as by the fake one.

If they refer to the real artist at all, it is in the third person rather than the first, as in this fieldnote excerpt in which a Buddy Holly impersonator exits the stage after his performance:

> When he finishes the song, he sticks his fist up in the air and says "God bless Buddy Holly and long live rock 'n' roll!" and runs off stage. The audience screams and claps and many people throw their arms in the air . . .

Even though he is impeccably costumed in Holly's signature 1960s suit with skinny tie and big black eyeglasses, even though he just finished singing Holly's signature songs like "Not Fade Away," "That'll Be The Day," and "Peggy Sue" using Holly's signature vocal hitch ("Muh-eye Peggy Su-uh-ue"), this impersonator ends his act by referring to Holly in the third person, semantically reminding the audience that he is not the real Holly. The audience responds enthusiastically anyway; this type of "perforation" of the membrane surrounding the impersonation game is ambiguous enough to present little threat to audience's interpretation of the encounter.

Performers use other tactics to remind the audience playfully that they are not the real thing, often diverging noticeably (and humorously) from a well-known part of the real artist's act. These tactics can put pressure on the impersonation frame by making its unreality difficult or impossible to ignore; but threats such as these can still be artfully incorporated into the ongoing experience of the game. In this fieldnote excerpt, an Elvis Presley impersonator does his version of a signature Elvis move—the wiping of the sweaty brow with a silk scarf that is then bestowed upon a lucky female audience member:

> Elvis flirts with another audience member, a middle-aged woman in front of whom he begins dangling the blue scarf he has around his neck. He keeps throwing it back around his neck and swishing it back and forth, then dangling it back in front of her, where she reaches for it and he then flicks it away from her again. He lets her almost grab it one last time, then flicks it away and instead of swishing

it around his neck, quickly opens his jumpsuit and sticks the scarf into the front, rubbing it into his armpit and then extricating it and delivering it to her. She takes it . . . but doesn't seem quite as game or excited as she had been a moment earlier. The audience laughs.

For a while here, both the impersonator and his audience work together seamlessly to reproduce a trademark Elvis moment. But the impersonator deviates from the script, soiling the scarf in a way the real Elvis never did. With this move, the impersonator reminds the audience that he's not the real Elvis—a "rule of irrelevance" (Goffman 1961:20) suspended for a moment by his humorous move with the scarf. It works, for that sweaty scarf is suddenly less enticing than it had been when everyone was playing along together. But the fantasy in which this performer is Elvis is at risk only for a moment; the impersonator returns to his role, and the incident is integrated into the game.

In the theater, audiences play the game largely by showing appreciation for the impersonator's performance, and there are a variety of ways to do this. For example, during impersonations of a legendarily sexy performer like Tom Jones or Elvis Presley, groups of mostly female audience members scream, yell, and reach out for the performer, responding to the impersonator just like the real artist's real audience might have done. In this fieldnote excerpt, the audience members respond to a Prince impersonator as if they were watching the real artist perform:

> The ladies right below me in the six-person booth are totally into this act, singing and pointing and gesturing during "I Would Die 4 U," which uses hand signs in the chorus, with Prince and all the dancers pointing to themselves, then making a little gun with their hands and touching it to their temples, then holding up four fingers, then pointing out to the audience—who are doing the same thing!

These audience members are enthusiastic accomplices in the impersonation game, participating with the performers in the hand gesture sequence that customarily accompanies this song at a real Prince concert. Here the audience and performers cooperate to maintain the sense of authenticity that helps sustain the impersonation frame. In addition, the hand gestures are fun, and allow the audience members to feel like participants or even co-performers in this act. Goffman (1961:42) would call this kind of easy, aligned collaboration within the impersonation frame "euphoric"; here, there is no incongruity between the "real" world and the world of the impersonation game.

There are other ways for audience members to play along besides merely being enthusiastic and participatory in their theater seats. Impersonators regularly select audience members to collaborate with them onstage; in these cases, the pressure is on the individual audience member to respond deftly in an onstage improvisation with the performer. Here, a Marilyn Monroe impersonator selects a man from the audience by asking him if he likes to "play games" while bringing him onstage:

> He says, "I love to play games," and she says, "That's what the President said." She then sits on his right knee, and he keeps his hands off her, lifting his right hand and waving it behind her so we can all see that he isn't touching her. She says that he is trembling all over and that he shouldn't be afraid, she won't bite. She blows on his head to "cool him off," and plays with his wispy comb-over hair until it's in a little spike atop his head, and says, "this is like cotton candy!" Then she gets up, removes his glasses, folds them and places them in her bosom, and starts breathily singing "My Heart Belongs to Daddy." She continues touching him, messing with his hair, folding and unfolding his collar, and unbuttoning his shirt so that his undershirt is visible, all while he flashes a huge grin and directs exaggerated winks toward the audience. When the song is finished, she kisses his cheek and sends him offstage—as he walks away she says to the audience, "Poor guy, he doesn't even know he's blind!" and he turns around to get his glasses back from her. She makes much of fishing them out of her dress, and finally puts them on his head as the audience laughs.

This Marilyn explicitly invites the audience member to enter into a game, and he explicitly agrees to play along. The action centers on Monroe's legendary sexiness, with the impersonator making playful but veiled references to Monroe's past with "the President" and treating the audience member to a bit of flirtation (to which he good-humoredly responds). The larger audience is also part of this game, and both the impersonator and her victim/collaborator orient to them and include them in the playfulness and joking occurring onstage. No reference, explicit or implicit, is made to the fact that Marilyn Monroe is dead; this selective inattention to a pesky real-world fact allows the game to continue without threat.

Finally, the play that occurs within the impersonation frame can continue even beyond the proscenium. In this fieldnote excerpt, a female audience member happens to be in the theater on the day that the real Sir Paul McCartney announced his plans to divorce his second wife, and she fights the crowd outside the theater to reach the McCartney impersonator at the end of the show:

> I see the pink sweats lady flirting with the Paul McCartney imper-
> sonator. She's smiling a huge goofy smile and saying "Well, you're
> not married anymore, so you're available, right?!"

She plays the game expertly, bringing information about the real McCartney into her interaction with the fake one, and in doing so, acknowledging his success at reproducing McCartney, even while the real Sir Paul is in England divorcing his wife. The real and the fantastic intermingle, even after the curtains have fallen.

Celebrity impersonator performances playfully straddle the line that separates reality from imitation. The impersonation game requires not just an accomplished impersonator, emblematic costumes, signature songs and skilled stagecraft. It also requires a cooperative audience, willing to collaborate with the performer in maintaining the celebrity impersonation frame. Shared involvement in the world created within the impersonation frame holds back the tide of external facts ("Elvis, Marilyn Monroe and Buddy Holly are dead";

"This guy is not the real Prince") that would ruin the game for all its players.

At impersonator shows, audiences can expect both authenticity and parody without contradiction; these qualities can coexist comfortably within the celebrity impersonation frame. Indeed, their apparent contradiction makes for an even more engrossing game, as the tension between the two introduces the risk of a problematic outcome, raising the stakes for all players. These seemingly contradictory qualities are key elements of impersonation, and of the reflexivity of this type of performance.

Breaking the Rules

Small deviations from the rules are manageable within the impersonation frame: Elvis gets laughs by swiping a scarf into a sweaty armpit, but those laughs are a temporary incident, balanced by the ongoing collaborative play between audience and performer. Sometimes, however, such an incident can present a much more serious threat to the engrossment of audience and impersonator within the impersonation frame. Risk to the impersonation frame and game can issue from a variety of sources, but when one party or the other cannot or will not play the game, the whole enterprise of impersonation is in peril.

Some celebrity impersonators face special problems in maintaining their role during their performances. This Rod Stewart impersonator, for example, deals cards at a casino gaming table, and cannot maintain the necessary vocal changes for his hours-long shift in a smoky, noisy gambling pit:

> . . . [F]or me, when I go to the tables, I'm not really doing Rod Stewart. I look like Rod Stewart, and all I do is just entertain the people. I don't try to put the voice on . . . A voice like Rod Stewart, he has a husky voice, and he's got an accent. And to do that with the noise going on . . . so it's like, "Well, Rod, where's your accent?" they'll say sometimes, and it's like "Yeah, if I did my accent you wouldn't understand me . . ."

His audience of card-players notices the absence of Stewart's trademark "husky" British accent—they evince a bit of what Goffman (1961:44) calls "uneasiness" or "dysphoria" about the world they think they have entered. They address their dealer-impersonator as "Rod," but they question who he "really" is. He, however, is clear about what he is doing: he can't keep up the accent under his current working conditions without making his speech unintelligible, a significant problem when one must be understood while calling bets. What this impersonator claims to be a necessary inauthenticity punctures the membrane surrounding his impersonation; even by his own admission, he's just a guy dealing cards in a Rod Stewart costume.

The engrossing world within the impersonation frame is maintained not just by performer and audience, but also by the backstage work of support staff and equipment. When there are technical difficulties during a performance, these elements of the external world are brought to the forefront, posing yet another threat to the game. In this fieldnote excerpt, Kenny Rogers and Dolly Parton impersonators experience a sound glitch during their act:

> They end the duet, and Kenny sings one song on his own. Then there is a snatch of different music before another song starts playing. Dolly barks toward the back of the house in a totally non-Dolly voice (no Southern accent) "You skipped a track!" but the music keeps playing. She barks it again, and at this point all the audience has turned around and is looking at the sound and light booth in the back, in the dark. The music keeps playing and this time Dolly (still in non-Dolly voice) whimpers, "You skipped my song."

The Dolly Parton impersonator breaks character noticeably under the pressure created by the technical problem. If this had been the real Dolly Parton, of course, any response she gave would be "in character," or at least part of an acknowledged Dolly Parton persona. But here, the emotional "flooding out" that results from the sound error takes the performer "out of play" entirely (Goffman 1961:55). She can neither control nor integrate the incident into her performance, and responds in a way that breaks the impersonation frame and stops the game altogether.

What happens when the audience cannot or will not play the game? The Neil Diamond impersonator in this fieldnote excerpt is moved to chastise his audience after they fail to participate in the "hands touching hands" sing-along during his opening song, "Sweet Caroline" and give a disappointing response to his greeting afterwards:

> He ends the song and talks to the audience: "Welcome to Branson, Missouri." No audience response. "Wow" he says, "Let's try that again. Welcome to Branson, Missouri!" There's a lukewarm "Yay" from the audience this time. He looks peeved. "Branson, Missouri, future home of Branson CSI—and it's looking like I'm the first victim."

This audience is not playing along, and the impersonator makes a frame-breaking comment as he reprimands them. His "Branson CSI" reference alludes to the superiority of Las Vegas as a show town (the original "CSI" is set in Vegas), and perhaps to the superiority of Vegas audiences in playing the impersonation game. By referencing Las Vegas—and the external world in general—in this way, he calls attention to the artifice of the whole game, effectively finishing it. But he blames the audience, implying that they have killed Neil Diamond. And symbolically, at least, they have.

Playing the game is essential to maintaining the celebrity impersonation frame. Impersonators and their audiences must collaborate in this game; without willing game-players, these performances break down, and both the celebrity impersonation game and the celebrity impersonation frame are threatened.

Conclusion

Goffman's (1961; 1974) notions of frame and game are useful in understanding the phenomenon of celebrity impersonation and the interactional negotiations that make it work. Performer and audience interact within a frame that allows for multiple layers of interpretation as impersonators move in and out of their celebrity roles. In addition, celebrity impersonation can be seen as a collaborative game, in which the audience and performers use the interactional boundaries of the impersonation frame to construct an absorbing world within which distinctive rules guide their interactions. In this world, impersonators playfully reference the unreality of their celebrity portrayals, and audience members finesse and integrate these references as part of the game. Rarely does such a reference truly threaten to end the game or break the frame, although this can happen. And while it is paid work for the performers, the audience plays the game for the fun of it.

Imitative performance genres, including but not limited to impersonation, may challenge some of the traditional ways of understanding theatrical performance and audienceship, and suggests that the distinction between "real" and "fake" is not black and white. They can coexist in celebrity impersonation, and, we suggest, in other settings as well. Within these specific interactional boundaries, the interplay of reality and simulation provides entertainment for those who play the game. Outside of the boundaries, however, the transposition of reality and fantasy might be cause for alarm, or for doubting the competence or sanity of the game player (Maynard 1991). Frame shapes the meaning of unreality and reality, in the theater and outside of it.

When celebrity impersonators perform, the borders between reality and fantasy become porous, as do the lines that separate fame from obscurity and performer from audience. Celebrity impersonation offers audiences the prospect that the "real" is both valuable (we desire an encounter with Elvis) and also flexible (Elvis is not available so an impersonator steps in). Within the impersonation frame, both performer and audience can play with reality, making a game of the fictions and mimeses of the impersonator's art. Fame is lampooned by its imitations, suggesting that "celebrity" is not necessarily the superior status (Evans 1998). Parody by impersonators neither rejects nor reveres a famous object, but turns it "inside out," presenting possibilities unimagined in more earnest performance contexts. Audiences move from spectators to co-performers—their agency is critical to an impersonator's authenticity as well as his or her artifice. The impersonation frame shapes an interactional context in which performer and audience playfully dissect and reconstruct fame, reality and performance conventions in the pursuit of entertainment. The impersonation game, then, is a social world in itself, where participants with access to particular interactional resources construct a distinctive reality together.

At the end of each "Stars on Parade" performance, all of the performers join Elvis onstage for a rousing rendition of "Viva Las Vegas." Shania Twain sings alongside John, Paul, George and Ringo. Buddy Holly holds hands with Britney Spears. A 1960s Aretha Franklin and a 1990s Prince sway back and forth together. Madonna smiles at Marilyn Monroe. This finale is beyond belief, bringing together stars from disparate genres, eras, and styles. Young and old, living and dead converge onstage, defying credulity. But it works. Within the impersonation frame, all of these alliances are not only possible, but they are the culmination of a game in which these very juxtapositions are part of the fun. Within the impersonation frame, the dead can live again and manifest fakes get the same attention as the real thing, creating and contesting notions of performance and ultimately, even the nature of "reality" itself.

5

"HOW DOES IT FEEL TO BE A STAR?"

IDENTIFYING EMOTIONS ON THE RED CARPET

"I love to win those things [Oscars]. Love it. The only part I don't like is the red carpet and getting a dress and walking around in high heels and holding in my stomach. I hate that."

Shirley MacLaine[1]

What are you feeling as you read this sentence? Perhaps curiosity or boredom? Did you bring to the reading of this chapter some frustration or nervousness about your hectic schedule? Is there a personal relationship causing you some anxiety or joy? Or are you content or perhaps feeling nothing of significance at the moment?

This chapter uses data on celebrities to take a close look at the processes by which we label (or "interpretively manage") how we feel. Figuring out what we feel is not necessarily a simple act, nor is it necessarily a task for isolated individuals. Would the answer you give to this question—how do you feel?—be shaped by *who* was asking and *where* they were asking, such as a teacher in a classroom, a friend at a party, or a romantic partner on a date? These are relatively "ordinary" occasions, whereas celebrities are regularly interviewed by entertainment journalists on the red carpet in front of millions of viewers. Nevertheless, we can study the way stars label their feelings in order to understand the social factors that shape the process of labeling feelings.

Conventional Emotion Management

In everyday life, people sometimes assume that emotions are biological conditions that shape our thinking and behavior. We say we "fall in love," that we become "struck with stagefright," that our "anger clouds our judgment."

While not necessarily disagreeing with that perspective, sociologists have often emphasized the opposite possibility: that emotions are subject to social and individual control. For decades, a central topic of sociological research on emotions has been the active ways that people *manage* their emotions (Lively 2006; Peterson 2006). The vast majority of this research has been on (what we call) "conventional" or "objective" emotion management. This research is interesting but is a bit different from the more interpretive emotion management that we will focus on later in this chapter.

Research on conventional emotion management shows how people can actively *create* their emotional states, especially in the following two ways. First, people can *surface act*, or put on a display of emotion that they don't necessarily feel (Hochschild 1983). For example, individuals may actively "work up" a display of gratitude in order to show appreciation for a gift that they are perhaps not very excited about. Most readers should be able to recall a time they enthusiastically said "Thank you very much!" even when they were given a present they really didn't want. Human beings can to a large degree control their facial expressions, tone of voice, and other indicators of their emotions, in order to navigate their interpersonal relationships. Customer service occupations often ask that workers at least *appear* happy and polite, even though the employee may be feeling irritation or impatience "on the inside."

The second "objective" or "conventional" way that people manage their emotions occurs when they try to change how they actually feel, rather than merely shaping how they appear to feel (Hochschild 1983). An example of this *deep acting* would be when individuals try to evoke a genuine feeling of gratitude by telling themselves "It's the thought that counts." Our companions may help us deep act, too. After a romantic relationship ends, our friends may tell us "there are plenty of fish in the sea" or remind us of the negative attributes possessed by our ex ("At least

now you won't have to deal with his annoying friends and bad breath!").
Even an employer or a co-worker may suggest "You should feel lucky to
even have a job!" as an attempt to encourage genuinely positive emotions
in an employee.

Many scholars have studied emotion-management strategies,
including how they are guided by cultural "feeling rules" and the tacit
requirements of various settings and occupations. Everyone from
athletes to detectives, medical students, prison inmates, salespeople, and
wheelchair users has been shown to engage in frequent surface or deep
acting. This research is important, but is not our main concern here.[2]

Interpretive Emotion Management

There is another way that people "work up" emotions beyond surface
and deep acting that has received less attention from sociologists. This
kind of emotion management consists of the processes by which people
"manage" feelings by *identifying instances of emotions*. The leading
assumption that guides this research is that emotional states are indeterminate; they must be interpreted because their meaning is not inherent.
Feelings do not come self-labeled but are talked into being. Emotions—
or claimed instances of them—arise as people discuss and debate feelings by themselves (alone in their own minds) or with others (in written
or oral communication). For example, whether someone has exhibited a
proper amount of gratitude is a topic someone might think about or
gossip about with others. Deciding whether a person is "grateful," "a bit
unappreciative," or "a total ingrate"—if not something else entirely—
involves meaning-making work. We call this form of work *interpretive
emotion management* (or IEM) since the focus of people's efforts is on
managing ideas or assertions about feelings, rather on the management
of bodily sensations or expressions (Harris 2010).

Treating Descriptions of Emotions as Claims rather than Reality Reports

In order to understand IEM, it is first necessary to develop some healthy
skepticism about emotional claims-making. Americans are sometimes
tempted to defer to individuals as having expert knowledge of their own
bodies. A popular song by Tom Petty echoes the cultural refrain "You

don't know how it feels to be me," which implies that only a person experiencing an emotion can authoritatively describe it. Interestingly, though, this lay theory does not always win the day. Sometimes people do try to tell *us* what we feel, as in "You're not in love—you're in lust!" Moreover, individuals can also question or contradict their own emotional self-assessments, as in "I don't know how I feel about this" or "I didn't know how happy I was until everything was taken away."

A common assumption underlying much discourse about emotions is that individuals can look inward to their own bodily states in order to observe and identify their feelings. This is questionable for a number of reasons (see Rosenberg 1990).

First, deciphering physiological reactions can be a complicated task. My heart is racing, adrenaline is flowing, my muscles are ready for action—am I excited, angry, or afraid? If my body is lethargic—am I sad, depressed, or merely relaxed? These are loose examples, but even the most careful scientists have a very difficult time deciding whether specific physiological conditions can be measured and correlated with specific emotions (Barrett 2006). The task is further complicated, in life if not in laboratories, since emotions can be mixed. A person may feel contradictory emotions in response to an experience: sadness and relief at the passing of a long-ailing parent, fear and excitement on a roller coaster, and so on.

People may speak confidently about their own and others' feelings, but in everyday life there is (arguably) little objective basis for this confidence. With an automobile, we can insert a dipstick and measure how much oil is in the engine. We cannot pause during a conversation, insert a dipstick down our esophagus, and then proclaim authoritatively that we "are full of rage" or that we "have no love left" for someone.

People may imagine language to be a proverbial emotional dipstick, assuming that our vocabulary provides an objective or at least sufficient means for understanding and characterizing emotions. But how do we know that our dipstick is designed accurately or adequately? Sometimes laypersons raise this concern when they portray their feelings as ineffable. For example, moments after Lee DeWyze won the 2010 American Idol singing competition, host Ryan Seacrest asked him "Can you describe the feeling inside you when I said your name?" In response, DeWyze claimed "No, I can't. There's no words to describe it." Not everyone would agree with DeWyze's extreme claim, but few would deny that language is imperfect. It is a human invention, and it evolves over time as people try to make sense of things and accomplish their goals. Consequently, different cultures develop different emotion vocabularies. English-speaking Americans have access to emotion concepts that some other cultures don't have, and vice verse. If we don't have the words "schadenfreude" or "fago" then perhaps we will be less inclined or able to identify feelings of malicious glee like German speakers or a particular mixture of compassion/love/sadness as the Ifaluk do (Lutz 1988; Russell 1991).

Emotional claims-making can be approached skeptically for other reasons as well—reasons that don't center so much on interpretations of bodily conditions. When people talk about their own (and others') feelings, they often seem oriented as much (or more) to external circumstances as they do to internal physiological states. Many speakers begin presentations with the claim "I am happy to be here" without appearing to engage in the slightest amount of reflection on their bodily conditions. Similarly, a companion may tell us "You're afraid of commitment!" or "You love controversy!" by looking not at our physiology but at our actions—perhaps our apparent tendency to break off relationships or to bring up politics during casual conversations. These assertions are interpretive inferences; a debatable emotion is attributed to a person based on observations of external behaviors.

IEM seems to be shaped by our interactional agendas, including the impressions we wish to make on others. The expression "I'm happy to be here" could be uttered to elicit a positive mood and reaction from an audience, while giving the impression that the speaker is someone who enjoys and is confident about his or her work. Similarly, "You're afraid of commitment" could be asserted by someone who is on the verge of being dumped, as a way of convincing a romantic partner to give the relationship another chance and/or as a way of protecting the dumpee's self-esteem, since the problem is portrayed as the result of the dumper's personality flaw.

Emotional claims-making cannot be taken as a simple reality report if it is (at least some of the time) shaped by such dramaturgical concerns. In general, it seems that IEM is subject to social norms as much as conventional emotion management is. Just as individuals surface act and deep act in order to make their outward expressions appropriate to the occasion, so too may individuals artfully craft their verbal descriptions. It is now culturally appropriate to proclaim that one is "proud" (e.g. of one's family) even though that emotion was in centuries past a "deadly sin" to be avoided. Currently, a parent cannot say "I hate you" to a child even in a calm voice—at least, not without the risk of negative sanctions from onlookers. Arguably, due to social norms, such a parent would feel pressure to *downgrade* such a negative description to "You are making me frustrated [or unhappy, etc.]." Similarly, parental norms may encourage descriptions of "fondness" or "liking" be *upgraded* to "love" for their children.[3]

One's source of employment may encourage or require that emotional claims-making take particular forms, which again suggests that we should not treat such assertions as simple reality reports. Is a restaurant hostess who exclaims "Welcome! We're glad you joined us today!" giving an objective assessment of her and her co-workers' feelings, or is she (at least as likely) making an attribution that fits the requirements of her occupation? Political candidate (now president) Barrack Obama once received criticism for describing a segment of the American population as "bitter." Performing his job well required developing a sensitivity to acceptable and unacceptable depictions of voters' emotional states; he had to watch how he spoke about feelings. Even a small-business owner may learn to reframe his or her emotions as "disappointed" rather than "pissed off," after his reaction to employees' performance is met with resistance.

Bracketing Emotions to Study IEM

For a variety of reasons, then, one can argue for the necessity of being skeptical regarding people's claims about emotions. There are always plausible reasons to question virtually any assertion about what a person or group is feeling. Any situation, and any emotional state, can almost always be described in different ways by different people (or even by the same person in a different context).

It would be a difficult if not impossible task to *prove* that one or more claims about an emotion are true or false. Since there is no objective basis for measurement—no emotional dipstick—there is arguably no way to authenticate claims. For the purposes of our research, then, we have simply oriented to emotional claims-making as an interpretive and interactive project. Through IEM, people give meaning to themselves and to others, and to past, present, and future situations. We treat IEM as always questionable, but we do not claim to know anybody's real feelings. We put that concern in "brackets" and set it aside while we analyze our data on celebrities.

Studying Red-Carpet Interviews

The Red-Carpet Scene

As they arrive at award shows, celebrities run a gauntlet of reporters from different media outlets, posing for cameras and talking with interviewers who are often celebrities themselves (such as comedian Joan Rivers, "American Idol" host Ryan Seacrest, or former MTV VJ Chris Connelly). These interviews are very brief (usually under 2 minutes), and can often seem rushed and unrehearsed, as if the interviewers don't necessarily know who will be stepping up to their microphone next and must *ad lib* their questions and conversations.[4] Red-carpet talk focuses on a limited set of topics: the movie or song for which the celebrity is nominated, their plans for future projects, their glamorous attire (and the bodies inside that attire), and their immediate moods and feelings about the evening's events. The interviewers habitually praise the celebrities (for their work, their outfits, their physiques), and celebrities customarily express gratitude for this praise and take the opportunity to promote their latest work. Celebrities also respond to questions posed by the interviewers about their emotions—questions about how they feel to be nominated and how they feel to be attending the award show. It is these questions and their responses that we will analyze in this paper.

We see celebrities on the red carpet as, among other things, emotional claims-makers who, through interview talk, construct labels for their feelings in a mass-mediated public setting. They do so within a set of constraints that govern red-carpet talk—including those noted in the prior paragraph, such as the limited set of topics and the focus on praise, self-promotion, and other public-image-enhancing approaches. On the red carpet the celebrity represents a product, or is a product him- or herself. Red-carpet interviews can be seen as being about selling that product, and hence must make a positive impact on millions of viewers in a matter of seconds. These constraints shape and drive red-carpet interactions. But red-carpet interviews occur within broader cultural vocabularies of emotion as well, and hew to the conventions and constraints that shape the emotion-management of non-celebrities as well as celebrities.

It is worth bearing in mind that all celebrities at award shows are "at work," and though viewers may believe that they are appearing "as themselves" on the red carpet, the likelihood is that they are there to promote themselves and their projects, and hence must be "on" and camera-ready when they step out of the limousine. In other words, appearances at award shows are a type of performance—not just in the Goffmanian (1959) sense in which we all perform, but literally, for those whose careers involve acting, singing or other kinds of performance. Celebrities are aesthetic and emotional laborers—they must present appropriate fronts both physically and emotionally when they are performing, and so it is not enough to merely look good while walking the red carpet. They display and talk about their emotions in strategic ways as well.

Data and Analysis

We taped and transcribed interviews from red-carpet interview shows airing before each of the following award shows aired during the 2007 award season: the Golden Globes, hosted by the Hollywood Foreign Press Association; the Screen Actors Guild (SAG) Awards, where actors union members vote on their fellow performers; the Grammy Awards, sponsored by the Recording Academy; and the Academy Awards or "Oscars," sponsored by the Academy of Motion Picture Arts and Sciences. We worked with nine sets of interviews because red-carpet interviews are conducted and televised by different networks—in this case, ABC, E! and TV Guide Channel.

Award Show	Date	Broadcast and Host(s)	Time	# of interviews
Golden Globes	Jan. 15, 2007	E! Network; Ryan Seacrest, Giuliana DePandi	1.5 hrs	44
		TV Guide Network; Joan and Melissa Rivers	2 hrs	33
SAG Awards	Jan. 28, 2007	E! Network; Ryan Seacrest, Giuliana DePandi	1.5 hrs	45
		TV Guide Network; Melissa Rivers	2 hrs	28
Grammies	Feb. 11, 2007	E! Network; Ryan Seacrest, Giuliana DePandi	1.5 hrs	42
		TV Guide Network; Joan and Melissa Rivers	2 hrs	43
Oscars	Feb. 25, 2007	E! Network; Ryan Seacrest, Giuliana DePandi	1.5 hrs	33
		TV Guide Network; Joan and Melissa Rivers	2 hrs	35
		ABC; Chris Connelly	0.5 hrs	14

These nine red-carpet broadcasts comprised 14.5 hours of video-taped material, and included a total of 317 celebrity interviews. A significant minority of these interviews (approximately 37 percent) involved multiple celebrities, as when one celebrity was accompanied by a celebrity co-star, bandmate, collaborator, or romantic partner. It is important to underscore here that the unit of analysis is the individual interview, not the award show or red-carpet broadcast itself. So, for the purposes of this paper, we analyzed 317 cases of celebrity red-carpet interview talk.[5]

One of the distinctive advantages of video data over audio is that there is more to work with than just spoken language. Facial expressions, tone of voice, gestures, body language, attire, and even the technical composition of the shots as broadcast on the television screen can be part of the data. We attempted to take these elements into account as part of our analysis, although our emphasis was ultimately on verbal accounts.

For some readers, red-carpet interviews may not qualify as "naturally" occurring talk. Such interviews do, however, occur within a set of distinctive and identifiable constraints that make them nicely analyzable for us as researchers. In the award show context, celebrities are recurrently and publicly asked to answer questions—such as "How are you feeling today?"—that most of us are asked in quieter settings. By conducting what is essentially a content analysis of televised interviews, we are able to treat celebrities' recurring red-carpet interactions as accessible, conspicuous examples of emotion-talk. As is the tendency with qualitative research, we expect that our analyses of the extraordinary case of red-carpet interviews will provide insight into more ordinary processes of emotion-talk in everyday life.

Analysis/Findings

The red-carpet walk is clearly a unique interactional setting featuring extraordinary interactants and an unusually large, mass-mediated audience. However, some of the patterns visible in red-carpet interview talk include strategies for the interpretive and collaborative construction of feelings that are undoubtedly generalizable to other settings and participants. These include the role of social context and audience expectations in shaping emotional claims; the need to account for unexpected or negative emotional claims; the role of other interactants in shaping emotional claims; and claims-making about the emotions of others. Celebrities and interviewers do all of these things on the red carpet, and we propose that the dynamics of these processes are equally applicable to ordinary interactants in more mundane situations.

Happy and Excited: Stock Responses

As in other, perhaps more routine social situations, there are expected or stock emotional responses for celebrities who walk the red carpet. The culturally-approved emotional vocabulary for award shows seems to require that celebrities announce that they are "happy" or "excited" to be there, and/or that they are "enjoying" themselves. Here, actor Leonardo DiCaprio responds to the interviewer's comments with a version of this stock response:

| Chris Connelly: | And what better way to begin than with Leonardo DiCaprio, a best actor nominee for "Blood Diamond" and a key part of the acting posse for "The Departed." Welcome back to the Oscars, Leo. |
| Leonardo DiCaprio: | Thank you very much. I'm really happy to be here tonight. Really excited about both these movies. |

Connelly didn't even have to ask "how are you?" to elicit the star's announcement about his emotional state; rather, DiCaprio was primed and ready to depict his feelings in response to Connelly's non-querying welcome. In the rest of the one-minute interview DiCaprio discusses the issue of conflict diamonds[6] and the pleasures of working with director Martin Scorcese, but before he can do that he displays the emotions required by his milieu. Celebrities on the red carpet are accountable to the emotional requirements of their local context, which include the expression of positive feelings like happiness and excitement. Within a red-carpet frame, these interpretations and expressions of emotions are expected.

While DiCaprio announces his emotions without being prompted by a question, in other interviews, the interviewer explicitly inquires into the celebrity's emotional condition:

| Greg Proops: | Greg Proops on the red carpet with Grammy winner, Enya. How are you today Enya? |
| Enya: | I'm <u>very happy</u>. Having just won a Grammy. My fourth Grammy, so I'm <u>going to enjoy</u> this evening tremendously. |

And here, host Ryan Seacrest elicits the stock response from members of the music group Pussy Cat Dolls by asking a slightly different question:

| Ryan Seacrest: | So have you prepared a speech? |
| Pussy Cat Nicole: | No. No. We're just <u>happy</u> just to be here. |

Like DiCaprio, both Enya and Pussy Cat Nicole declare that they are feeling happy to be present—at the award show or on the red carpet, or both. In this context, "I'm happy to be here" is a clichéd response, like "I'm doing fine" would be in a more mundane encounter. Even from the perspective of common sense, the status of such an utterance as a simple reality report is suspect, as such phrases can be overused to the point of having little real meaning. "I'm excited" is also a kind of rote or hackneyed phrase in this particular social context. However, to express emotions other than happiness or excitement is to reframe the red-carpet walk as a negative experience, something that is seen only rarely. Awards shows are presented as glamorous and thrilling events, especially to those watching from home, and celebrities deliver stock responses that support these expectations.

Neither Happy nor Excited: Negative Feelings

While expressions of excitement and happiness are the benchmark emotions for celebrities on the red carpet, the possibility remains that not all stars "actually" feel that way, and some stars are willing to talk about negative emotions in red-carpet interviews. While admitting to a negative emotion is rare, some celebrities may compare the way they feel now (positive) with the way they felt at past award shows (negative), making seemingly contradictory emotional claims in one interview:

Joan Rivers:	Okay, we are here with LeAnn Rimes and her husband Dean. And you are both a nominee and a presenter tonight.
LeAnn Rimes:	I am a nominee and a presenter ah—this is <u>exciting</u>.
Joan Rivers:	You were 14 years old—you have had enough—when you, ah, first—.
LeAnn Rimes:	It's completely different from 14 to 24. It was 10 years ago and it's a completely <u>different feeling</u> and I ah actually get to <u>enjoy</u> the festivities. I'm not a kid kinda being toted around everywhere.

In this interview, singer Rimes claims to be excited tonight, but looks back on her first Grammy ceremony 10 years prior as "completely different." While she can "enjoy" the ceremony she is currently attending, the past ceremony was presumably not enjoyable. By comparing past and present award show experiences, she suggests that not all red-carpet walks are exciting, enjoyable, or happy. Singer Sarah Kelly does something similar:

> Greg Proops: Welcome back, Greg Proops here on the red carpet with the divine R&B artist, Sarah Kelly. How are you darling?
>
> Sarah Kelly: Hi, very good thank you. [*Brings palm to chest in a gesture of modesty*]
>
> Greg Proops: This is your second time at the Grammies, <u>how are you feeling</u>?
>
> Sarah Kelly: It is my second time and it's so much *easier to enjoy* this time around. The last time it was all a big whirl [*swirls right hand around above head*], so <u>I'm really just enjoying myself</u>.
>
> Greg Proops: A little bit <u>more grounded</u>. Did you eat something today?

Like Rimes', Kelly's statement that it's "easier to enjoy" the second time around suggests that not all celebrities experience award show attendance as emotionally positive, and her use of "big whirl" in this context (in combination with a swirly hand gesture) hints at something overwhelming or disorienting about the experience. In fact, these comments also suggest that some of the very people who preceded Kelly and Rimes on 2007's red carpet, claiming to be happy and excited, might return in 2008 and revise those claims through similar comparisons.

Not being happy or excited, or at least expressing happiness or excitement, is so rare and non-normative as to require an account on the part of the celebrity. In this interview with Melissa Rivers, actor Paul Giamatti scorns his monster indie hit from the prior year, "Sideways," instead of talking up the current year's movie, "Cinderella Man":

Melissa Rivers:	. . . Paul Giamatti. You're nominated this time—[*overlapping talk*]—as a supporting actor.
Paul Giamatti:	Yeah. Yes I am.
Melissa Rivers:	For "Cinderella Man."
Paul Giamatti:	That's correct, ma'am.
Melissa Rivers:	And last year was "Sideways."
Paul Giamatti:	Yes. Correct.
Melissa Rivers:	Do you really actually remember or care to remember anything about wine?
Paul Giamatti:	No, I never knew a damn thing about it. Hate wine. Hate the wine people. Hate the whole damn thing.
Melissa Rivers:	And you can say that now it's a year later.
Paul Giamatti:	Well I can say it. It's a year later and everybody's forgotten and now I can cut loose with that.
Melissa Rivers:	And we were just talking about how bizarre this whole scene is.
Paul Giamatti:	Well, you know, yeah. It's interesting—it's a circus though. It's a bit of a circus.
Melissa Rivers:	Is it different this year now that it's sort of like, you know, you get your sophomore effort on the red carpet.
Paul Giamatti:	It is a little but I feel a little bit—yeah, I feel like an old hand. I'm not so green anymore.

Giamatti professes his hatred of all things wine-related (the topic of "Sideways") and accounts for this confession by noting that, after a year has passed, "everybody's forgotten" and he is free to "cut loose" with this shocking admission. In addition, Giamatti calls the commotion of the red carpet a "circus," implying that because he is "an old hand" he can call it as he sees it. In this case, Giamatti's complaints are encouraged by Rivers. Even so, these cantankerous comments run counter to the overwhelmingly positive dispositions displayed by other celebrities and effectively reframes Giamatti's red-carpet experiences as unpleasant burdens rather than happy, exciting opportunities.

Actress Maggie Gyllenhaal also goes against the grain and expresses a negative emotion on the red carpet—fear. She is asked to account for this feeling by interviewer Ryan Seacrest:

Ryan Seacrest:	So are you attending tonight? Just watching the show.
Maggie Gyllenhaal:	I'm presenting.
Ryan Seacrest:	Presenting. You're on stage in an official capacity.
Maggie Gyllenhaal:	Yeah. <u>I am actually pretty scared</u>.
Ryan Seacrest:	Are you really?
Maggie Gyllenhaal:	Yeah.
Ryan Seacrest:	Alright what are you <u>scared</u> of? Why are you <u>frightened</u>? Let's break it down. Let's overcome your <u>fears</u>.
Maggie Gyllenhaal:	Well, I've watched the Academy Awards before and, like, taken people apart. Kind of, like, slayed them.
Peter Sarsgaard:	Like at home eating popcorn.
Maggie Gyllenhaal:	Yeah. I'm a little <u>scared</u> of that. I'm a little <u>scared</u> of tripping. I've got, um, feathers on the bottom of my dress.

Gyllenhaal volunteers her feelings of fear without being asked by Seacrest; in response, he initially expresses doubt ("are you really?"), and then proceeds with a partly playful attempt to analyze the source of Gyllenhaal's fear. This type of detailed accounting for one's emotions is rarely entered into on the red carpet, especially when the emotions expressed are positive (excitement, happiness). By confessing to being scared, Gyllenhaal opens the door for Seacrest to call for an explanation, which she then provides. Interestingly, her reasons for being scared center on her awareness that an immense audience will be watching and evaluating her, and that she may do something embarrassing or be criticized by viewers as she performs her award show duties. This suggests a reframing of the experience of award show presenters for the television audience: why, in such a situation, wouldn't nearly everyone be afraid?

In this interview excerpt, Leonardo DiCaprio reveals a possible explanation for why so few celebrities admit to feeling anxiety, fear, or other negative emotions on the red carpet:

Leonardo DiCaprio: We're all <u>nervous</u>.
Ryan Seacrest: Are you <u>nervous</u>? You don't look it at all. You're totally calm and collected.
Leonardo DiCaprio: It's inside. [*Appears to open his tuxedo jacket and place his hands on his chest*] It's the acting.

Not only does DiCaprio admit to feeling nervous (and to locate that feeling within his physical body), he also reminds his viewers and interviewer that he (and, presumably, each of the other performers on the red carpet) is "acting," and that his "calm and collected" exterior is only a pretense.

Happy? Excited? Responding to Interviewer Suggestions

When interviewers ask celebrities about their feelings, the questions themselves can provide conceptual resources for the respondent—in other words, interviewers' questions can shape the answers they receive from celebrities by pre-framing the meanings of the events and their appearances at them. These questions can be seen as "coaching" the celebrities to constitute their emotions in a particular way, and frequently these questions assume what was discussed in the prior sections—that celebrities are "excited" or "happy"—and lead them to talk about that excitement or happiness in their responses.

Celebrities sometimes accept questioners' vocabularies as sufficient terms for making sense of their emotional states. Here, interviewer Proops suggests and assumes that excitement is the appropriate, expected emotional response from Joan Baez as they talk on the red carpet at the Grammies:

Greg Proops: Who are you <u>excited</u> to see when you're here?

Joan Baez: Well, I'm introducing the Dixie Chicks and because of their brief history and my long one I am, um, very <u>excited</u> to hear them.

Greg Proops: I am too. I think they are exceedingly brave.

Here, the question is quite specific—"who are you excited to see when you're here?"—and Baez responds by echoing the emotional term used by the interviewer. Proops assumes excitement, and Baez assents and confirms it (after which Proops agrees with Baez, further reaffirming excitement as the proper response). She also adds an explanation for her emotions that does double duty—it accounts for her feelings of excitement by drawing a link between herself and the Dixie Chicks as social critics, and it promotes her appearance at the Grammies as a presenter.

Excitement isn't the only emotion suggested by interviewers, though. Here, interviewer Seacrest suggests to actress Gwyneth Paltrow that such excitement can also be overwhelming to attendees as well:

Ryan Seacrest: I was talking to—well basically everyone who was walking in. And at this point on the carpet people still have that look of being <u>overwhelmed</u> when they arrive. This carpet is really so deep and wide and crazy. Is it always <u>exciting</u> to be at something like this?

Gweneth Paltrow: Yes it's always *nice* to come and see old friends and trying to focus on the task at hand. Try not to get too <u>overwhelmed</u>.

Paltrow takes up Seacrest's language, but without necessarily supporting his assumption that there is a negative aspect to the excitement of award shows. Her utterance attempts to reframe a potentially "overwhelming" event and turn it into something "nice." She implies that it is possible to enjoy the heightened emotional state Seacrest suggests, or at least to avoid getting "overwhelmed." This utterance may serve a dual purpose of advising other red-carpet walkers at the same time as Paltrow talks herself into the feeling.

Seacrest also goes beyond the cliché of "excitement" in this interview with Oscar host Ellen DeGeneres, suggesting that she might feel nervous or uncomfortable as she prepares to take the stage:

Ryan Seacrest: How are you doing? You've done the Grammies, you've done the Emmies; it's the first time you're doing the Oscars.
Ellen DeGeneres: Yes.
Ryan Seacrest: Are you <u>nervous</u> about it or are you <u>comfortable</u> doing all these big shows?
EllenDeGeneres: Ummm ... No, I'm <u>comfortable</u> because I've done it a lot but of course I'll be <u>nervous</u>. I mean it's live all over the world and so right before I walk out there I'm going to be <u>nervous</u>. Right now I'm <u>excited</u>.

Here, DeGeneres is initially asked an open-ended questions about "how" she is "doing," but does not respond directly, obliging Seacrest to suggest some additional feelings—nervousness, comfort/discomfort—to induce her to talk about "how she is." At this point DeGeneres does respond to the questions about her emotions, and uses Seacrest's terms to do it, pausing before affirming the language he uses by using it herself, while also negotiating a bit about the meanings of the feelings he suggests. While she claims that prior experiences hosting award shows will mean that she is "comfortable," she will still be "nervous" because of the live worldwide broadcast (similar to the anxiety expressed by Maggie Gyllenhaal in an earlier section). And of course, she also declares that she is "excited," as must be expected in this context.

Finally, interviewer DePandi, at the SAG Awards with actor Jackie Earle Haley, encounters direct resistance to her suggestion that Haley is "excited" to be there:

Giuliana DePandi:	Alright, joining me now is Jackie Earle Haley who is nominated tonight in the best supporting actor category for "Little Children." How <u>excited</u> are you right now?
Jackie Earle Haley:	I am just, <u>just beside myself</u>. I'm <u>freaking out</u> [*DePandi laughs as Haley shakes his head, rolls his eyes, and smiles sheepishly*] and I'm <u>nervous</u> and I'm <u>scared</u>.
Giuliana DePandi:	Are you <u>nervous</u>? Are you <u>scared</u>?
Jackie Earle Haley:	Yeah.
Giuliana DePandi:	Well, you know, and you're also nominated for an Oscar. I mean, this has been such an unbelievable year for you.
Jackie Earle Haley:	It, it, <u>I feel like I'm dreaming</u>. I, I really do. So, don't wake me up, whatever you do. [*Laughs*]

Haley admits to feeling something less glamorous than the "excitement" commonly claimed on the red carpet. He is "nervous," "scared," and "freaking out," and he must contradict DePandi in order to make these claims. By brushing aside the interviewer's suggestion to reframe his experience as "exciting," he is swimming against the red-carpet tide; by admitting to negative emotions, he is even more unconventional; and by demonstrably appearing to feel them, he is a rare specimen indeed. Perhaps because it has been decades since he has been in the Hollywood spotlight, Haley is more frank—or at least less compliant than other red-carpet walkers.

Conversations such as these demonstrate that celebrities' emotional responses can be portrayed as more complex than just "excitement" or "happiness," involving different and/or multiple emotions. In addition, celebrities may allow the interviewers to effectively frame their feelings for them by adopting the language of the questions in their responses, though others may attempt to negotiate the labels that are applied to their feelings. Also, when interviewers suggest feelings that celebrities are unwilling to claim, those celebrities must contradict interviewer suggestion in order to profess their "real," negative emotions. Finally, admitting to negative emotions (fear, anxiety) may be easier to do once the interviewer has suggested them. Indeed, interviewer suggestion may make it easier to frame emotions of all sorts, as it allows the interviewer to lead and the celebrity to follow.

Happy and Excited for You: The Emotions of Others

The emotional states of the celebrities themselves are not the only focus of labeling and claims-making on the red carpet; the emotions of others are also brought into play as celebrity and interviewer chat. Here, actress Jamie Pressly speaks for her "My Name Is Earl" co-star, Jason Lee, in an interview with Ryan Seacrest:

Ryan Seacrest:	How <u>excited</u> are you to be here tonight? I mean, we've had a chance to talk about the last couple of years and your career, and this show is just, it's, it's a fantastic show and it's allowed you to do some great things. How does it feel to be up here nominated tonight?
Jaime Pressly:	It's really, really <u>exciting for, uh, both Jason and I</u> to be nominated, um, by our peers, because, you know, uh, they're the hardest, the hardest critics to, uh, to win over and the fact that they chose us to even be in the, you know, in the group is pretty amazing. So, <u>we're really excited</u> to be here tonight.

Not only does Seacrest suggest a stock emotion for Pressly to declare herself to be feeling, Pressly immediately claims that emotion both for herself and her co-star, framing this excitement as something they can feel together. Lee is not present, but Pressly still speaks in terms of "we," asserting that she and her co-star share the same feelings about their respective nominations.

Co-stars aren't the only people about whom celebrities make emotional claims. Here, Leonardo DiCaprio speaks for his date—Mom—after Seacrest suggests how she may be feeling:

Ryan Seacrest:	Who have you brought? Who have you come with?
Leonardo DiCaprio:	My mom. But she's—
Ryan Seacrest:	Where's mom?
Leonardo DiCaprio:	She's strolling around here. Not into the whole press thing.
Ryan Seacrest:	Does she get <u>excited</u> about coming to these things, or she's been so many times she's used to it by now.
Leonardo DiCaprio:	She <u>loves</u> it, man. She <u>loves</u> this whole party. She <u>loves</u> the night. She <u>loves</u> being here. She is more <u>excited</u> than me right now . . .

Seacrest invites speculation about the emotions of the absent Mama DiCaprio, and son Leo carries forward by making claims about her emotions ("she loves being here"), despite the fact that she is not present to speak for herself. As with the celebrities themselves, it seems that celebrity mothers are also assumed to be happy and excited about their attendance.

In another instance, the emotions of unnamed mass others (an entire city in Texas) are confidently identified by both the interviewer and the celebrity. As Joan Rivers questions Eva Longoria Parker about the training regimen that she uses to keep in shape, Longoria Parker notices that a note about her previous participation in a beauty pageant has been typed on an off-camera cue card:

Eva Longoria Parker:	[My workout is] an hour and my trainer just picks whatever . . . Oh my God you put "Miss Corpus Christi USA." [*Laughs*].
Joan Rivers:	Yes.
Eva Longoria Parker:	That's <u>funny</u>.
Joan Rivers:	I went to Corpus Christi and all they talked about was you. I was there the day after the hurricane. They <u>couldn't care less</u> they had no houses—they talked about you. [*Eva laughs*] I <u>love</u> you. It's great to see you.

Eva Longoria Parker:	Thank you.
Joan Rivers:	<u>Corpus Christi loves you.</u>
Eva Longoria Parker:	Aww, I hope I'm making them <u>proud</u>.
Joan Rivers:	Trust me <u>they love you</u>. Melissa, back to you.

Here, Joan's assertion that "they love you" fits the interactional frame of the red-carpet context nicely. It compliments Longoria Parker, helps to maintain a positive mood, and links together (improvisationally, like jazz) the sequence of statements that resulted from the decision to include "Miss Corpus Christi USA" as a potential talking point. Of course, the people of Corpus Christi might say they "feel" a great many other things about Longoria Parker—indifference, envy, approval, disgust—if they were asked. And clearly, many such citizens would say they "care" more about the loss of their own homes to a hurricane than they would about a famous actress. But award shows are in large part focused on celebrity adoration, so "love" and "pride" are the feelings that are imputed here.

Nobody Cares if I'm Happy or Excited: Interviewers' Emotions

Finally, in only a few interviews are the tables turned, with the celebrity inquiring into the feelings of the interviewer. In an interview with "Desperate Housewives" star Teri Hatcher, Joan Rivers is drawn into an uncharacteristically mundane exchange of pleasantries with the actress, and must finally resort to an atypical question to elicit more than just bland niceties from Hatcher:

Joan Rivers:	How are you?
Teri Hatcher:	I'm good, how are you?
Joan Rivers:	I'm just great.
Teri Hatcher:	Nice to see you again.
Joan Rivers:	Certainly. Nice to see you. Some year, huh?
Teri Hatcher:	Yes. It's been an amazing year.
Joan Rivers:	And what has changed most in the year?
Teri Hatcher:	Wow. Ummm ... opportunities and, uh, maybe just sort of a <u>sense of peace, of feeling like I have a</u>

job that's not instantly going away and, um,
you know, but the ground of things like friends
and family, that doesn't change. But it's been an
amazing year.

Here, Hatcher treats the interaction as an ordinary one, at least
initially, and asks Rivers about her own feelings as if they were conversing
in an ordinary setting. This makes Hatcher seem somewhat uncoopera-
tive given the red-carpet context, though it might be perfectly acceptable in an office hallway or over the backyard fence. Not until Rivers
asks a non-standard question (about what has changed for Hatcher
during the past year) does Hatcher provide a more detailed response.
Rivers' efforts to re-focus the interview on Hatcher reveal that the
celebrity respondent is the one whose feelings matter most within the
red-carpet frame, and that how the interviewer feels is not the desired
focus of the interaction.

In another interview in which the tables are turned, actress Emily
Blunt and singer Michael Buble try to ask interviewer Seacrest how he
is feeling:

Michael Buble:	So how are you doing tonight? Does anybody ask you how you're doing?
Ryan Seacrest:	Nobody cares how I'm doing. I'm on the air—you care?
Emily Blunt:	We care. I never got to meet you before.
Ryan Seacrest:	Only heard about—so are you guys—wha—what—you guys engaged?

An off-camera Seacrest sounds flummoxed by this question, stating
that "nobody cares" about his feelings, and implying that being "on the
air" means that how he feels is moot and uninteresting. Despite Blunt's
insistence that they do care, he stumbles ahead with a gossipy question
about the couple's romantic status, taking the focus off his own feelings
and placing it back on those of the celebrities. While both celebrities
and interviewer are "on the job" in these interactions, it is assumed that

viewers are only interested in the emotional claims and displays of one category of performer.

Given this, it seems only natural for comedian/actor John Krasinski ("The Office") to make fun of the whole red-carpet interview scene by turning the tables on his interviewer, taking hold of the microphone himself and interviewing her instead. Here, he uses a common strategy already discussed above—suggesting an emotion for interviewee Giuliana DePandi to assent to:

John Krasinki:	. . . How <u>excited</u> are you tonight?
Giuliana DePandi:	I'm very <u>excited</u>, uh, "The Office" is nominated, so I'm very <u>excited</u>.
John Krasinki:	It's a pretty good show. Um, what are you wearing?
Giuliana DePandi:	I'm wearing Louis Verdade, thank you so much for asking.
John Krasinki:	It looks beautiful. Show it off
Giuliana DePandi:	Oh. OK.
John Krasinki:	Do a little, little turn. [*She turns around and becomes entangled in a previously unseen web of AV wires attached to her back*]
Giuliana DePandi:	Alright.

Krasinski's prank reframes the interview with DePandi as its focus. Even though DePandi has agreed to play along, she still has a hard time figuring out how to respond when the questions are directed at her. While she immediately responds with the stock phrase "I'm very excited," she can only explain why in reference to the "interviewer's" show, rather than citing any of her own reasons for being there. She also pauses ("Oh. OK.") when asked to show off her own dress, something she regularly asks of others. Krasinski has to prompt her to "Do a little . . . turn" in order to become a sartorial object herself.

Celebrities use the resources provided by the extraordinary interactional context of the red carpet to frame and shape their emotional claims-making. But that does not mean that their emotional instantiation strategies are unique. All of the dynamics of emotion talk discussed in this analysis are generic enough to be observed in other interactional settings. Using "stock" emotional vocabulary suggested or required by the setting, and negotiating with or allowing fellow interactants to suggest how one should be feeling, are common social processes. These interactional dynamics should be visible beyond the red carpet as well as on it, as should others, including accounting for negative, unexpected, or dis-preferred emotional claims, making claims about the emotions of others, and minimizing one's own emotional expressions to focus on those of others (especially in the context of paid employment). Celebrities are one of the few groups who are well-compensated for their skill at crafting emotions on the job but, beyond the red carpet, the strategies they use to label and identify emotions are undoubtedly deployed by non-celebrities as well, making them worthy of continued analysis.

Conclusion

There is a very large literature on the strategies people use to "manage" their emotions as bodily sensations and expressions. Following Hochschild (1983), a great deal has been written about the techniques that individuals use in order to evoke or suppress emotion at work or in their private lives (Lively 2006; Peterson 2006). In this chapter, we have attempted to contribute to a smaller body of research that focuses on an arguably equally important topic: how people "work on" *ideas or assertions* about emotional states (see Gubrium 1989; Staske 1996). By conceiving of emotions as labels that are applied to indeterminate states of affairs, this somewhat more interpretive approach to "emotion management" (IEM) centers on descriptions of emotions—how feelings are imputed by and to self and others in interaction.

We believe that red-carpet interviews provide an opportune site for the investigation of this type of emotional instantiation. However, our use of this data source begs the question of its relevance to more mundane locations and interactions. Our loose observations of everyday life, combined with our reading of the previous literature (e.g., Edwards 1999; Staske 1996), lead us to conclude that there is nothing remarkably unique about the emotional claims-making behaviors that celebrities (and their interviewers) engage in. Red-carpet interviews are indeed "special" in that they are televised to potentially millions of viewers. And it is true that celebrities are often wealthy, highly-trained performers—two traits that may affect their capacities and tendencies to manage impressions and persuade audiences.

However, by thinking in terms of generic social processes (Prus 1996), it is possible to discern the common (if not utterly ordinary) aspects of IEM. We have focused on several such processes, including directly imputing emotions to oneself or to other individuals and groups; influencing others' emotional claims by offering candidate labels in the form of a question; and shaping emotional claims in anticipation of audience expectations (and accounting for any deviations from those expectations). Each of these ways of thinking and talking about emotions appear and are experienced by actors within a wide variety of interactional frames.

These sorts of behaviors are truly generic rather than context-specific. Routine, everyday situations that all readers should be familiar with—such as being posed the question "How are you doing?"—regularly involve emotional instantiation. More specific inquiries—such as "Are you feeling alright?" or "Are you excited to graduate?"—guide the process by providing candidate labels. And answers to such questions may vary depending upon one's audience (e.g., a group of friends, a parent, a teacher, a potential employer, a therapist) and upon one's interactional goals (e.g., eliciting approval, amusement, sympathy, respect).

In addition, celebrities themselves can serve as role models for their audiences, for better or worse.[7] Celebrities' charisma, beauty, talent, and wealth are potential sources of power over others, and audiences may want to emulate their favorite stars as a result. As they give interviews on the red carpet, celebrities' outfits and hairstyles inspire copycat designs; and if this is true for celebrity style, it may be true for styles of verbal and emotional expression as well. Watching celebrities talk about their emotions on the red carpet can provide instruction for audiences on how to express and constitute their own feelings.

These observations, along with our data on celebrities and the existing literature, suggest that emotions are not necessarily the private or personal experiences that they are sometimes assumed to be. Like other experiences (Gubrium and Holstein 1995), emotions are public entities in that they are "shared" and concertedly "worked on" in diverse settings that may be far removed from our "intimate" relationships with close family and friends. People use cultural resources to label feelings in context-sensitive ways (Gubrium 1992). Classrooms, courtrooms, therapy sessions, office boardrooms—in these settings and others people may be guided towards assorted understandings and depictions of emotional states according to the distinctive frames of meaning in the setting (Goffman 1974). "Celebrities on the red carpet" can thus be seen as merely one more location where putative feelings are interpretively and interactively worked up and managed for diverse audiences and purposes.

6

"WHEN DID YOU KNOW THAT YOU'D BE A STAR?"

ATTRIBUTING MIND ON THE RED CARPET

As we saw in the last chapter, celebrities' feelings are a popular topic on the red carpet.[1] Interviewers unabashedly ask stars to "reveal" their emotions, via indirect and direct questions (such as "How are you doing?" and "Are you excited to be here tonight?"). Celebrities tend to respond to the interviewers' coaching by labeling their feelings in a context-sensitive manner. We argued that this sort of emotional claims-making is not dissimilar to that which occurs in everyday life. Americans routinely create instances of emotions by asserting that they or their companions are happy, proud, envious, jealous, "pissed off," and so on. Each label gives meaning to indeterminate situations and tends to serve certain goals in social interaction, such as avoiding conflict, eliciting respect, or creating humor. Thus, the apparently "private" experience of emotion can be analyzed as a social project: the interactive application of cultural categories.

In this chapter, we examine another aspect of human experience that—like emotion—may at first seem "internal" to individuals but is also a product of social interaction. In America (as in most Western cultures), a common assumption is that individuals possess "minds" which enable them to imagine possible futures, make plans, direct their own actions—in short, to *think*. Americans frequently assert or imply that individuals are or should be rational, in the sense of being self-aware and exercising conscious control over their own behavior (to the best of their ability). Thus, it makes sense that in everyday conversations, in classrooms, in opinion polls, in court testimony, and in other arenas, people regularly "self-report" about what goes on inside their heads—as in "I was very surprised to learn that . . ." or "I have always been a firm believer in . . ." When questioned about their motivations for committing laudable or untoward actions, people regularly avow and disavow mental intentions, such as "That was an accident" or "Sorry—I was drunk when I did that."

As counter-intuitive as it may sometimes seem, these "first-hand" accounts of thought processes—like claims about emotional states— can be seen as strategic interpretations rather than simple reality reports. There is always more than one way to depict the inner workings of one's mind, and a different choice might create different meanings and serve different interactional purposes. Moreover, people do not limit themselves to self-reports; they regularly make claims about the minds of others. It is commonplace for individuals to impute mental qualities and predilections to their companions, as with "You don't think about anyone but yourself" or "She is as sharp as a tack."

In this chapter, we explore the topic of "constructing minds" using the same data as we did in Chapter 5 on emotions: transcriptions of 317 televised red-carpet interviews which took place prior to nine major awards shows. We examine the mental claims-making that celebrities and interviewers engage in, during the red-carpet interactions that take place just prior to award shows. The red-carpet scene again provides a highly observable and accessible venue for witnessing the collaborative production of meaning, this time focused on the concept of mind: celebrities' putative thoughts, predictions, motives, and related phenomena.

We begin this chapter with a brief review of the literature on mind, to demonstrate the broad relevance of this topic and to distinguish the particular brand of "constructionism" that we apply here.

Conventional Approaches to the Creation of Mind

To study the "social construction of mind" is almost to turn constructionism back upon itself. This is because a fundamental premise of (much) constructionism is that people *interpret* things rather than experiencing reality directly or "in the raw." Since meaning is not inherent, constructionists argue, people must actively classify that which they encounter. For most constructionists (e.g., Blumer 1969; Schutz 1970), this interpretive process takes place (to a large degree) in and through people's minds, as they interact with others or think things over in solitude.

Constructionists acknowledge that biology—especially the brain—is central to thinking, but they assert that mind's origin and application are profoundly social. Without instruction into the language and practices of a particular culture, human beings do not think and act as competently and variably as they do (Berger and Luckmann 1966). Rare "feral" children who are raised in relative isolation have been found to lack language and age-appropriate reasoning abilities (Blumer 1981; Davis 2006). In contrast, normally socialized individuals are taught how to think, and what to think. In primary socialization, children internalize the basic assumptions and values of their society (as in "public nudity is embarrassing"); in secondary socialization, adults continue to acquire new ways of thinking (as in "It is very prestigious for a scientist to publish an article in that journal").

Constructionists tend to argue that human beings act based on what things mean to them (Blumer 1969). For example, whether an individual enjoys eating worm tacos, cow muscle, or tofu depends in large part on the cultural meanings s/he has learned to apply to food. Since mind is such a crucial aspect of human behavior, many constructionist scholars give it a prominent place in their work. They tend to portray thinking as a topic that *researchers* should conceptualize, study, describe, and explain.[2]

Studying Mind as a Claim

Along with conventional approaches to mind, there is another (but less frequently pursued) route that some constructionists take (e.g., see Edwards and Potter 2005; Gubrium 2003). This alternative stand of research sets a different agenda, by asking: What if "mind" was studied as a *claim* rather than an actual entity or process that guides behavior? What might researchers learn by focusing on the assertions that different people (in different contexts) make about the inner workings of their own and others' minds?

By re-conceptualizing the topic of "mind" in this fashion, some researchers have tried to contribute different insights about the social dimensions of cognition. They have tended to do so by focusing on "questionable" or controversial attributions of mental phenomena, in order to highlight the contradictory meanings that can be given to putative manifestations of mindful (or mindless) behavior. In this section, we discuss two examples of this type of research. Then we relate mental claims-making to more routine circumstances before turning to our data derived from celebrity interviews on the red carpet.

Can Animals Think?

According to some constructionist theorists (Mead 1934; Meltzer 2003), only human beings can "think." Since the "lower" creatures do not possess language and a sense of self (the argument goes), they cannot engage in the internal dialogue that constitutes thought. A squirrel may gather nuts for winter, but it would be an anthropomorphic fallacy to infer anything other than instinct from this action; the squirrel does not imagine a cold, barren winter and tell itself to plan ahead (see Mead 1934:119). Similarly, two dogs may bark at each other, but their "conversation" is instinctual rather than minded. Their behavior is not "symbolic" because the canines react directly to each other's sounds and actions; unlike human interaction, there is no intervening process of interpretation whereby interactants evaluate and assign meaning to vocalizations and gestures (Blumer 1969).

The sociological study of animals has grown rapidly in recent years (Irvine 2008), and much of this work challenges this rather stark contrast between human beings and animals. Clinton Sanders (2003a; 2003b; 2007) in particular has argued repeatedly that animals are more similar to human beings than previous scholars have suggested; both human and non-human animals may be capable of assigning meaning, making plans, conceptualizing strategies, engaging in play and trickery, and other minded behavior. Sanders notes that in everyday life people often attribute various degrees of mind to their pets, and these attributions seem to "work" for them. For example, it is not uncommon for dog owners to claim that their pets act in a purposeful and strategic manner: dogs are said to remind their owners that it is time to eat or take a walk; cats are sometimes described as "leaving a present" for their owners when they deposit a dead rodent on the door-step (even though the gift might not be particularly well-received!). Based on these interpretations, owners may alter their behavior towards their pets, in order to get them to understand that their behavior needs to change. People may view their companion animals as less intelligent than human beings, but they do frequently assert that their pets can "figure out" and "remember" (and yet, like humans, still choose to violate) the desired customs and rules of the house.

What is important for our purposes in this chapter is not the ultimate status of animal minds; the issue of whether dogs, cats, squirrels, and other creatures can *think* is interesting but not (for us) essential to answer. From our purposes, the lesson we take from Sanders' work is that it is important to recognize the frequency with which attributions of mental states are made as well as the consequential meanings that can be generated by those attributions.

For constructionists, any single object, behavior, or situation can be described in many different ways. If we begin to apply this premise to minded behavior, then we can study all attributions of mind—whether animal or human—as claims making and meaning making. After all, a romantic partner bearing flowers may be described as "Acting guilty about something," "Trying to curry favor," "Behaving very thought-fully," or "Just doing something out of habit." The possibilities are as variable as the claims that could be made about a cat delivering a dead rodent to the door step—except that the romantic partner can (more verbally) endorse or resist candidate descriptions.

Do Some People Possess "Criminal Minds"?

While animals cannot be asked to describe (verbally) their own thoughts and intentions in much detail, people usually can. However, individuals' claims to self-understanding are not simply accepted in social interaction. Mental self-reports can be disputed even among those who are able to speak clearly on their own behalf—especially, but not only, among those who are perceived to be abnormal or deranged. Our second example of research on the interpretive construction of mind—preliminary to our study of celebrities—thus comes from the areas of crime and deviance.

In court, the putative "reasons" or "motives" that drive people to commit an action are often a central concern. Legally, it can matter a great deal whether an assault was impulsive or premeditated, or whether an employer fires a worker for reasons of poor performance or due to sexual or racial prejudice. Judges and jurors must make determinations of guilt, innocence, and liability based on the mental claims-making of lawyers, defendants, witnesses, and others (e.g., see Scheppele 1994). Even after being convicted and incarcerated, a criminal may not find the real or proverbial "file" on his or her mental status to be closed. Parole boards and prison officials may look for evidence of self-awareness and genuine personal growth on the part of offenders when considering the possibility of early release (Radelet and Roberts 1983).

In one particularly interesting study, Fox (2001) observed a prison reha-bilitation program for violent offenders entitled "Cognitive Self Change" (CSC). Convicts who elected to participate in the CSC program could potentially receive a reduced sentence. The guiding philosophy of CSC was that, while crime might be traced to many contributing factors, ultimately it is criminal mindsets that produce criminal actions. In the end, a person must choose to act in an unlawful manner. Given this philosophy, CSC staff were trained to teach prisoners to recognize certain criminal thought patterns in their past and current behavior, and to cultivate new ways of thinking. By developing the ability to identify problematic thoughts within themselves (the CSC theory goes), offenders should be able to channel their thinking and thus their conduct in more acceptable directions.

Despite the incentive of an early release, some prisoners rejected CSC staff's depictions of their conduct. Not all convicts agreed that their conduct was due to a criminal mindset, and they would cite other reasons for their behavior, such as contextual factors (e.g., self-defense or peer pressure). Prisoners who challenged CSC portrayals of their biographies were told by staff that they were engaging in "distorted concrete thinking" (Fox 2001:180). In a group session, if an inmate complained about poor prison conditions or improper behavior by the guards, CSC staff asserted that this too was evidence of a criminal mindset. If another prisoner confirmed the same complaints, their claims were depicted by CSC staff as simply indicating that they shared a flawed way of thinking—such as perceiving themselves as victims or being prone to anger (Fox 2001:179). Thus, in this setting, mental claims-making creates contested meanings that can be very consequential for individuals' identities and futures.

Mental Claims-Making as an Ordinary Occurrence

Work by Sanders and by Fox provides two examples of research on conventionally "questionable" imputations of mind. It can be enlightening to study attributions of mental states in overtly controversial circumstances, as these authors have done. However, once one begins to think "generically" (Prus 1996) about the topic of mental claims making, its ubiquity becomes readily apparent. People routinely assert and deny states of mind, and it may be helpful to think more broadly about this subtle yet pervasive practice before examining its occurrence among celebrities on the red carpet.

Everyday conversations are filled with apparent self-reports such as "I'm surprised to hear you say that," "I'm concerned about you," "I thought that movie was fascinating," and "I'm a firm believer in . . ." Individuals also regularly assign mental traits to their companions, as in "He's not the sharpest tool in the shed" and "I wish I had your confidence and self-assuredness." Mind's actions, abilities, and failures are also frequently invoked, as in "I get your point" or "You don't know what it's like."

Attributions of mind are so ordinary that the topic may seem unremarkable or trivial. Some scholars (and lay-persons) may assume that individuals are describing (literally) self-evident facts when they express what they think or believe; others may assume that mental claims-making is too trivial too consider at length. However, an interpretive constructionist approach—such as the one that we take in this chapter—holds that assertions about mind are an important way that people create meaning, and that such meanings can be a formational elements of people's identities and actions. Mental claims-making is an interpretive act that can have consequences both large and small, as with other forms of claims-making. Some interpretive researchers find the topic worthwhile regardless of whether the setting is a high-profile congressional hearing, a focus group, a couple's counseling session, or a simple conversation between friends.[3] In this chapter, we will examine the topic via the venue of celebrity interviews on the red carpet, and will attempt to draw parallels with less dramatic settings.

Celebrities' Claims-Making about Mental Phenomena

Red-carpet interviews provide an opportune venue for collecting data on attributions of mind, and not only because the conversations are televised and easily accessible. In this setting, stars are pointedly asked to explain their "thoughts" and describe their "decision making" regarding their careers and other related topics. Since their statements are broadcast for millions of spectators—including fans, family and friends, co-workers and employers, journalists and commentators, among others—the "logic" of stars' claims are open to extensive scrutiny by viewers.

All of us are held accountable for the intelligibility and plausibility of our mental claims-making. For example, it could be risky to claim "I have no idea why I married my spouse" if one's betrothed is participating in the conversation. However, red-carpet interviews provide a situation where accountability is especially pronounced, given the large and diverse audience that will evaluate celebrities' statements and actions. Nonetheless, despite the highly public nature of the pre-award show interviews, we would assert that celebrities' mental claims-making is basically parallel to that which occurs in everyday life.

There are two conversational topics that are predominant on the red carpet and that tend to consistently generate mental claims-making. Celebrities are frequently asked to respond to the questions "How did you become involved with this project?" and "When did you know that your project would be successful?" The first two sections of our findings highlight the attributions of mind that occur when stars answer these questions.

In the subsequent two sections of our findings, we document the ubiquity of mental claims-making by looking at two common conversational practices: the third section examines how interviewers and celebrities attribute thoughts to other persons and entities; the fourth section focuses on attributions of mind that pervade humor and small talk.

Choosing Projects

In everyday life, individuals are commonly asked to explain their behavior, especially when their actions are considered exceptionally good, bad, or unexpected. When the question arises—"Why did you do that?"—it encourages people to formulate some kind of a coherent explanation, whether humble, apologetic, self-congratulatory, humorous, or defensive.

On the red carpet, celebrities' apparent successes and failures are often well known. Stars carry reputations into the conversations based on their past work, but interviewers can also selectively inform or remind viewers about particular aspects of entertainers' careers. An interviewer may allude to the fact that a singer has been "nominated for X and Y" or "recently recorded the number-one hit 'X'." Sometimes stars are asked to comment on their apparent flops and disappointments, as when an interviewer inquires about a cancelled television series or a critically and commercially unpopular film. Usually, though, the red carpet interaction is designed to be energetic and upbeat. Interviewers seek out those entertainers who are currently receiving nominations and awards for their work.[4] In these positive interactions, interviewers ask celebrities to recall those fateful moments when they decided to participate in the successful project at hand. Consider this excerpt:

Chris Connelly:	You've got so many roles to choose from. Why was that the right role to pick in "Blood Diamond"?
Leonardo DiCaprio:	You know it's very rare within the Hollywood studio system that you get to do a film that has somethin' pertinent about the world to say. It's a really relevant topic, conflict diamonds, and I really wanted to endorse that. And hopefully more movies like that will come out of the Hollywood studio system.

In the excerpt above, DiCaprio explains his participation in "Blood Diamond" as the result of his assessment of the film's strong moral message. He claims that he chose to act in the film because it said "something pertinent" about the world, and also because he wanted to encourage the studio system to produce similar films in the future. Of the multitude of factors that may lead to an actor's participation in a film, DiCaprio suggests that a mental state—his desire to participate in and encourage socially relevant films—was the principle cause. Arguably, this claim serves many purposes or leads to many benefits. First, it asserts something positive about his project, which may increase its appeal to viewers (and lead some to go see the film in theaters, purchase a DVD copy, tell a friend about it, etc.). DiCaprio could be described as actively promoting the reputation and economic success of his film—something that many entertainers would be personally inclined (if not contractually obliged) to do. Second, DiCaprio's claim asserts something positive about his own character. His purported decision-making process "reveals" that he is a serious person who wants to participate in (and encourage) meaningful projects rather than empty entertainment.

Questions about the selection of projects often presume a great deal of agency on the part of stars. The assumption is that actors, musicians, and other entertainers have much discretion regarding the directions their careers take. Celebrities frequently affirm the assumption and focus their responses (as DiCaprio did) on the positive features that they purportedly deemed attractive about a project.

"Agency" is something that speakers can "work up" or "work down" as they formulate their accounts. In everyday life, it is not uncommon for individuals to claim that exterior events "forced" them to think, feel, or act in a particular way—as when people say "You make me so confused!" or "That is fascinating!" Celebrities, too, can accentuate or minimize the agency they exerted in selecting their work projects. In the excerpt below, a documentary film-maker claims a relatively simple decision-making process lay behind her selection of a project: the topic and events were so compelling to her and her partner that they simply "had" to do it:

Joan Rivers:	There are so many wonderful documentaries that are out there tonight up for Academy awards. One is called "A Recycled Life." The director is here, Leslie Iwerks. And tell us what it's about, it's an amazing story.
Leslie Iwerks:	"A Recycled Life" is about the thousands of people who've been living and working in the Guatemala City garbage dump over the last 60 years.
Joan Rivers:	And it's generational they—born and die and born and die in the garbage dump.
Leslie Iwerks:	Cycle of poverty over six decades.
Joan Rivers:	What made you get involved in this?
Leslie Iwerks:	Um, Mike—Mike and I were producing a project on the Maya down in Guatemala, and we came upon the dump. <u>And it touched our hearts and we just had to tell the story.</u>

Iwerks suggests that her heartfelt reaction drove her to pursue a documentary project. Arguably, this claim is at least partly strategic in that it gives listeners the impression that they "have" to see the film and be moved by it.

Similarly, in the next example Mark Wahlberg begins his account by (at first) completely removing any self-agency from his decision-making process, and in so doing formulates an account that casts his film project in a very positive light.

Ryan Seacrest:	And "The Departed". <u>Tell me how you chose that film.</u> Obviously a great decision and a hell of a cast, but how did it come down for you?
Mark Wahlberg:	The—<u>I didn't choose "The Departed." It chose me.</u> When Marty Scorsese calls, you say "Okay where do I show up" and usually you ask how much you have to pay to be a part of a film like that, but they actually wanted me to be in it. I grew up in that neck of the woods and I have a lot of experience with the police

> in Boston. Not usually the right side of the law, but
> uh, you know, it was nice to be able to—to be in my
> comfort zone, in my wheelhouse, especially to work
> with Marty. [From 07 Golden Globes on E]

Wahlberg's account first attributes cognition to an entity without a brain: the film selected him. But this statement is probably not intended to be taken too literally (though this comment is a form of mental claims-making on our part as analysts!) and is likely made for dramatic effect. Wahlberg then suggests that the appeal of working with director Martin Scorsese made his decision a very easy one. He mentions that his experiences as a delinquent youth in Boston drew him to the film's topic, making it a comfortable role (and possibly explaining Scorsese's decision to select him). If viewers are inclined to patronise "The Departed" and interpret it as a superior film, then Wahlberg has provided them with numerous reasons to do so. His explanation of his decision-making process invokes the presence of an outstanding director and an actor whose background resonates with his part in the film.

Predicting Success

In everyday life, people tend to believe it is important to understand good and bad actions in light of the knowledge an actor held at the time. When we purchased a present, were we confident that our spouse would love it or hate it? When we finished the last carton of milk, did we know that a roommate had not yet eaten breakfast?

On the red carpet, the meaning of celebrity conduct is similarly deemed dependent on "what they had in mind" at the time. Choosing a project, bringing the work to fruition, and celebrating its completion at an awards show can all mean different things, depending on what one thinks (or claims to) about one's work. Interviewers especially want to learn about stars' original predictions concerning the possibility of aesthetic or economic success.

In the excerpt below, Eddie Murphy claims his participation in a film was accompanied by an utterly consistent confidence about its prospects of being well-received.

Lisa Ling: So "Dream Girls" is the most nominated film tonight. <u>Did you expect that it would be as commercially and critically acclaimed?</u>

Eddie Murphy: Absolutely. <u>When we were doing it, I felt like we were doing something special.</u> Yeah, <u>I thought it had everything.</u>

Murphy's claims about his mental states give the impression that his film's success is a welcome but not surprising or overwhelming experience for him. In contrast, musician Cee-Lo Green claims no knowledge that his album would do so well on the charts, which accentuates the impression of surprise and astonishment.

Ryan Seacrest: I heard the entire album, track to track to track. It's pretty fantastic. <u>Did you know when you made it that this was a home run?</u>

Cee-Lo Green: <u>I didn't. I didn't.</u> Um, I must say, uh, there's a bit of a divine intervention. I mean, that's what I consider it as. It's been such a miraculous year for me, like in a 13-year career. Like, people don't know that I've been around for that extent of time. So, I'm pretty fortunate and privileged to be here right now with you.

Neither Murphy nor Green challenges or undermines the interviewers' claims about the success of their projects; they could have directed attention to effective marketing campaigns, to lingering imperfections in their work that they'd remedy if they could, or to other related concerns. Instead, they accept the interviewer's premise and address the issue of "whether they knew" they were making hits. Murphy's answer conveys to listeners a high and utterly consistent confidence in the quality of his product (perhaps at the risk of appearing "cocky"). In contrast, Green's response appears more humble (claiming in effect that he had "no idea") but still attributes an extraordinary if not supernatural quality to his work.

In the next excerpt, Hugh Laurie carves out a middle position between possessing complete confidence and having no idea about the outcome of one's work. Widely known for the cantankerous character he plays on television, Laurie explains his past predictions of commercial success from the perspective of a seemingly hard-nosed realist.

> Brigitte[5]:   So "House" is doing very well, <u>did you expect it to do this well?</u>
>
> Hugh Laurie: Uh. No, frankly. No. Umm, I, I thought it would be good. I always loved the script, I loved the character, and I thought we'd have the chance to do a really good show, but good doesn't always mean successful, in fact it often doesn't. Um, and of course the odds against you, any time you do a new show on TV, uh, the casualties, it's so brutal you know. So many shows don't work. Even really good shows don't—don't succeed. But no, I never really imagined I'd be here three and a half years later still doing this. It's—it's amazing to me. I continue to marvel at it.

In this response, Laurie covers many bases at once. He asserts a confidence that his project would be "good" in many respects, but he avoids the appearance of cockiness by invoking a somber assessment of the difficult odds facing TV shows. He ends on a positive note, sounding more like Cee-Lo Green as he asserts that his show's success amazes him continuously and ongoingly. However, Laurie's assertion that he "never really imagined" his show's long life-span is noteworthy for the inclusion of the qualifier "really." This adverb seems an effective way to highlight surprise while warding off criticism from listeners; many viewers might suspect that the possibility of success is something that crosses virtually every entertainer's mind (at least briefly) during the course of undertaking a major project.

Attributing Thoughts to Others

In everyday life, individuals not only make claims about their own mental states; they make explicit and implicit assertions about the thinking of others as well. For example, people attribute mental capabilities to others through statements such as "I'm sure you realize that . . ." and "You're like an elephant—you never forget!" They also attribute mental incapacities to others through statements such as "You just don't understand!" and "Have you lost your mind?"

Celebrities, too, make claims about the cognitive status of others. As in everyday life, this helps them craft their own identities and navigate sensitive conversational topics. In the excerpt below, interviewer Seacrest asks why some award presenters are more successful than others in their attempts at humorous dialogue. This puts comedian Tina Fey in the position of having to express an authoritative opinion and implicitly raises the issue of whether she will put her knowledge into practice during the subsequent show.

Ryan Seacrest:	Welcome back to the Beverly Hilton, the center of the Golden Globe entertainment universe. This is Ryan Seacrest along with Tina Fey who's presenting tonight with David Spade.
Tina Fey:	Yes. David and I are presenting.
Ryan Seacrest:	What is the key to making it work? Because sometimes these things flaw—they—they fall flat.
Tina Fey:	We—David and I are hoping to just get in there and be quick and get out. Because <u>everyone wants to see the awards. They don't want to see a big play.</u>
Ryan Seacrest:	Brevity's the key when you're presenting.
Tina Fey:	Brevity, absolutely.

Fey's response to Seacrest's provocative question has the benefit of attributing a humble mental state both to herself and to her fellow presenter: she and Spade are merely "hoping to just . . . be quick and get out." Fey bolsters this assertion with a corresponding claim about the mental predilections of the audience: "everyone" is there to see the awards more than the playful repartee of the presenters. Both claims are, of course, challengeable. If pressed on these points, it seems likely Fey would admit that she was also hoping to get a laugh from the audience (i.e., that she was not simply seeking to "be quick and get out") and that some members of the audience may watch award shows for the presenters' repartee as much (or more than) for the actual awards that are distributed. Her response, however, does allow her to appear humble, to lower expectations about her upcoming performance, and to escape the awkward position that Seacrest's question placed her in.

In the next excerpt, a writer, editor, and popular culture commentator Peter Castrow responds to an interviewer's request to discuss the reunion of the band "The Police," who were scheduled to perform the opening song at the 2007 Grammy Awards.

> Castrow: A lot of people are wondering why is Sting doing this because he is a bizillionaire. He just woke up one day and said you know what it's time. Called the other guys and the other guys were in shock because they've been wanting to do it for a really long time. And that was it. Sting said let's go and everybody goes.

In this pithy response, Castrow casts himself as a knowledgeable reporter and assembles a terse causal analysis by making several attributions of mental states. First, he suggests that many people "are wondering" about Sting's behavior, and that these people view Sting as a person who would be motivated primarily by financial considerations. Second, Castrow depicts Sting's decision-making process as simple yet mysterious: the musician simply woke up and said "it's time." Third, Castrow portrays the other band members as uniformly "in shock" due to their consistent and longstanding preference to reform the band, in comparison to Sting's reticence.

Obviously, more extensive and divergent accounts could be provided if Castrow were asked to elaborate, if one or more of the band members were asked to speak for themselves, if the interviewer challenged or doubted one of the interviewee's statements, and so on. However, under the auspices of the red-carpet setting, Castrow's succinct account suffices. He confidently distills the putative thoughts and motives of many different people into a five-sentence narrative.

Humor and Small Talk

As we have said, interpretive scholars argue that situations do not have inherent meaning; similarly, neither do the words that people use to describe those situations (Blumer 1969). Most, if not all, of our vocabulary is difficult to define clearly, and the same words take on different meanings in different settings (as when "ball" can mean a football, a baseball, a baseball pitched outside the strike zone, a formal dance, an enjoyable experience, a testicle, etc.). It takes *work* to create and understand intelligible sentences, as well as to apply them to ambiguous contexts. Consequently, the participants to any conversation must conscientiously connect unclear words to unclear situations as they pursue their interactional goals (see Heritage 1984; Liberman 1999).

In humorous interactions, such meaning-making work continues but is given a whimsical spin. As Michael Flaherty (1984) has argued, the process of creating jocular meanings converts "reality work" into "reality play." For example, in offices and via email accounts, people share and laugh at small-town newspaper headlines like "Kids Make Nutritious Snacks" because of the divergent meanings that can be attributed to them. Are the children assembling healthy refreshments or are the children themselves being fashioned into nourishing treats? The former interpretation is generated by reality work, the latter by reality play.

In this section, we will document the prevalence of mental claims-making by highlighting its role in humor and small talk. We will focus on a single extended excerpt, where the participants make numerous explicit and implicit claims about their own and others' mental status. Each rapid-fire claim postulates a non-serious attribution of motive or cognition, creating playful meanings about the participants' personalities and relationships. Though insightful readers can likely find additional examples of mental claims-making in this rich excerpt, we will limit our discussion to six items (which we have numbered in brackets). Giuliana DePandi is the interviewer and "Weird Al" Yankovic is the celebrity. Part way through the interview they are joined by red-carpet walker, actor Gary Dourdan from the television show *CSI*.

DePandi: Weird—I mean, Al, you've won three Grammies.

Yankovic: I have. Thanks for noticing.

DePandi: Where are they?

Yankovic: Uh, I have them on top of my TV set <u>to pick up better reception</u>. **[1]**

DePandi: Oh, okay. You didn't bring them with you tonight?

Yankovic: I didn't. <u>I was going to, just to impress you</u>, **[2]** but I left them at home.

DePandi: <u>It would have worked</u>. **[3]**

Yankovic: Would it? [*Laughs*]

[. . .]

DePandi: How many millions, and millions, and trillions did you make off of [the song] "Eat It"?

Dourdan: The one you did of Kurt Cobain, [that] was hilarious.

Yankovic: "Smells like Nirvana." Thank you man. Thank you.

Dourdan: Hilarious.

Yankovic: Thank you.

DePandi: <u>Don't try to avoid my questions</u>. **[4]**

Yankovic: Oh ah, twelve trillion zillion. Twelve—

DePandi: That's how much money you made off of "Eat It."

Yankovic: Yes. Twelve trillion zillion.

Dourdan: How come she's always asking about money, man?

Yankovic: What is it with you and money?

Dourdan: <u>Gold digger</u>. **[5]** [*Laughs*]

DePandi: Where's Kanye when I need him. You know <u>I inspired that song</u>. **[6]**

In item **[1]**, Yankovic suggests that he keeps his past Emmy awards on top of his television, in order to increase his signal reception. This is obviously an unlikely scenario for such a wealthy celebrity, who likely subscribes to cable or satellite television in addition to having a separate room or display case for his trophies. The playful statement creates a humorous image of a trophy-antenna, pokes fun at awards in general, and gives off an impression of humility.

In item [2], Yankovic claims that he had originally planned to bring his trophies in order to impress the interviewer, DePandi, before changing his mind. Both the original and the subsequent mental state— the planning to carry three Emmys and the decision against it—are playful deviations from the reality work of mental claims-making. There is an unresolved tension that also adds to the levity: is Yankovic perhaps flirting with or mocking DePandi?

DePandi carries the joke further in item [3], seemingly accepting Yankovic's statement as (faux)-flirtatious. She claims that seeing Yankovic carrying the trophies would indeed have impressed her. In this hypothetical response, DePandi attributes a silly perspective to herself: she playfully suggests that she is the sort of person who would form a favorable opinion about a celebrity who carried his old trophies to a new award show.

Later in the conversation, Yankovic is asked two nearly simultaneous questions—including DePandi's sensitive inquiry about finances, which he neglects to answer. Subsequently, in item [4], DePandi assigns a motive to Yankovic. She claims that he has purposefully avoided her question, an assertion that lightheartedly impugns the singer's character.

In item [5], Yankovic and Dourdan turn the tables and ascribe a non-serious motive to DePandi, by suggesting that her apparent interest in money stems from her materialistic tendency to forge romantic relationships exclusively with wealthy men ("gold digger").

In item [6], DePandi accepts the negative attribution but turns it into a positive one by taking it a step further. She playfully asserts that she provided the inspiration to the artist Kanye West, who had recently released a popular song entitled "Gold Digger." Here the joke is twofold, at least: DePandi seemingly endorses the notion that she is a crass and calculating gold digger who would only be interested in affluent men, while suggesting that she is so influential that she provoked a famous artist to decide to record a song about her.

Throughout the conversation, Yankovic, Dourdan, and DePandi play-fully ascribe motives and thoughts to themselves, to each other, and to outside parties. They create silly identities and actions that clearly do not exist, while simultaneously working to establish their own (more conse-quential) reputations as witty and accomplished, yet self-deprecating, public figures. The excerpt demonstrates how "Who thinks what?" can be a central issue in even the most casual or silly conversation.

Conclusion

Although mental concepts (such as thinking, planning, imagining) form the foundation of much constructionist theory, scholars most often employ "mind" as an explanatory resource. Mind is treated as a real ability that is nurtured and shaped through social interaction. Researchers attempt to document the diverse perspectives, worldviews, or mindsets that individuals acquire via their participation in various social worlds.

While we endorse this approach in many respects, in this chapter we have attempted to contribute to a smaller body of work that moves constructionist research towards the examination of mental phenomena as interpretations. Mental claims-making can be studied as yet another meaning-making process, one that is on par with claims-making about any sort of situation, including other "internal" states (such as emotions or physiological sensations) and "external" conditions (such as politics, war, or poverty).

Despite the rationalistic tendencies of Western culture, an interpre-tive constructionist approach holds that individuals do not have unme-diated or unbiased access to the workings of their own minds, let alone the thoughts of others. Instead, people creatively interpret and artfully depict what "goes on" when someone (or some animal or thing) engages in putatively mindful or mindless behavior.

We used data from televised celebrity interviews to document the pervasive, seemingly unremarkable attributions that produce putative instances of thoughts, reasons, predictions, impulses, and so on. We have also tried to show how stars and their interviewers seem to craft interpretations of mind that are sensitive to context and audience. These short-hand depictions of mental states seem tailored to be pithy and positive, to promote projects and bolster reputations in front of a large and diverse audience.

In everyday life, few conversations are filmed and televised for millions of spectators. Yet celebrities' mental claims-making does not seem radically unfamiliar; instead, it seems to be merely another incarnation of a generic process that occurs in casual conversations everywhere. For example, students (like celebrities) are asked to explain the projects they choose—from their selection of a major, a career path, a romantic relationship, a party—and when they knew that things would work out well or poorly for them. The "beliefs" and "decision making processes" they attribute to themselves can be seen as selective and interpretive accounts that are tailored to accomplish particular goals, including navigating interactional constraints and managing the impressions of the audience.

As we noted in Chapter 1, some scholars see celebrities as remarkable for their narcissism and for their commodification. These themes can certainly be read into this chapter. However, our main goal here has been to demystify celebrities and their social interactions. The sense-making obligations and practices on the red carpet are (in many ways) not extraordinarily different from those who have never experienced their 15 minutes of fame.

7

CONCLUSION

STUDYING THE INTERPRETIVE AND INTERACTIONAL DIMENSIONS OF CELEBRITY AND FAME

As we explained in Chapter 1, many scholars and pundits treat celebrity and fame as matters of pathology or commodification. Celebrities are portrayed as narcissists whose fame is based on trivial accomplishments. People who purposefully consume celebrity have been portrayed as capitalist dupes, buying into messages of individualism and consumerism promoted by media coverage. Fans' interest in stars' lives and products is said to be a cause and consequence of dysfunctional and exploitive relations in society.

In this book, we have not set out to challenge these perspectives, but rather to add to them in order to build a more comprehensive sociology of celebrity. In the previous five chapters, we have attempted to demonstrate (and thereby promote) analyses of celebrity and fame that center on the meanings that celebrities and their fans create in social interaction, rather than on analytical arguments about pathology and commodification.

We take social interaction in any realm to be worth studying on its own terms. Human interaction is fascinating, if approached with the right mind-set. A single strip of conversation can be full of drama, movement, and meaning, regardless of (or in addition to) its potential connection to economic, historical, or cultural trends. In the substantive chapters of this book, we discuss scores of specific, concrete examples of (celebrity-centered) human behavior, which is one way of showing that we respect interaction enough to give it serious attention. If human beings are construction workers who build meaningful worlds, then it is important to examine in some detail the actual work they do.

At the same time as we treat social interaction as "special," we also have sought to de-mystify interaction within the area of life that we have examined. Interactions involving fame and celebrity can be approached as merely another set of occasions where people create meaning as they do things together. By focusing on the generic, transcontextual features of human behavior (Prus 1996), it is possible to see strong parallels between the realm of celebrity and more mundane settings. This demystification of celebrity does not require that differences are necessarily ignored, but it does encourage us to attempt to build on and contribute to various traditions of interactional research.

In this book, we have tried to build on one fundamental assumption and three lenses that can be derived from the interactionist literature: meaning is not inherent; social interaction is governed by norms and cultural understandings (microstructuralism); norms and understandings are somewhat malleable and emergent (negotiated order); human beings are constant claims-makers whose descriptions create order out of ambiguity (discourse analysis). In what follows, we highlight these themes as a way to summarize *Stargazing* and draw parallels between research on social interaction in general and in the realm of celebrity.

Meaning is not inherent

Human behavior is complex and difficult to explain. Any given behavior can be attributed or traced to a wide range of factors (Berger 1963). We are guided by external constraints, such as existing opportunities (or lack thereof!) in the job market. Internally, our behavior is shaped by the perspectives we are socialized into, such as any religious values (or again, lack thereof!) that we learn to live by. And then, alongside external and internal constraints, human beings arguably have free will—the ability to choose from a range of options or do something unexpected.

We recognize that many factors impinge upon any behavior, and we don't intend to reduce interaction to a single source. However, we do agree with Blumer (1969) that human behavior is to a large extent meaning guided. For example, many Americans try to lose weight because they have been encouraged to view "excess fat" as unattractive or unhealthy.[1] If being somewhat heavy were defined in more positive terms, such as a sign of wealth or sexiness, then many dieters would likely act differently. The meaning of body fat is not inherent, and interpretations of its meaning shape people's actions. The same is true of virtually all aspects of our lives. Collectively or individually, people could choose to define any thing in many different ways, and the meanings they give things tends to shape the lines of action they pursue. Experts and pundits may try to dictate what things mean—as when a medical doctor "educates" the public on the "real" health implications of body fat—but people can form and act on their own understandings and priorities.

The ideas that "meaning is not inherent" and "meanings inform our actions" have pervaded most subfields of Sociology. For example, the majority of scholars recognize that there is no single correct definition of "family" (Harris 2010). Many in the U.S. seem to endorse the "mom-dad-kids" model of family, but in practice families take many shapes and sizes around the world and in the U.S. Regardless of how the U.S. census, conservative pundits, or a Sociology textbook defines family, individuals and groups formulate and act on their own understandings. Someone may decide to interpret a step-parent or an adopted sibling as not a "real" relative, while another may treat a pet cat as a full-fledged family member. In some families, such interpretations can shape behavior dramatically, such as influencing who participates in important gatherings and rituals (e.g., gift exchanges). And even within daily family life, the meaning of any particular action or event can be interpreted in different ways (Gubrium and Holstein 1990). If a sibling spills grape juice on your favorite sweater or (ouch) sleeps with your fiancé, it could be interpreted as an unforgivable cruelty, an understandable lapse in judgment, just desserts for a prior injustice, and so on. Pundits or experts may confidently proclaim the naturalness of certain forms of family or of certain interpretations of events, but if they do so then they may not be fully recognizing the diverse meanings that people can give to their family relations and to their daily experiences.

In *Stargazing*, we have taken this same basic approach. As we explained in our introductory chapter, we depart from the scholarly trends of incorporating celebrity into scholarly tales about pathology or commodification. While defensible, prior work in these veins has under-appreciated the meanings people live by. Instead we have approached celebrity as another realm of interaction where (a) meaning is not inherent and (b) people act based on what things mean to them. When watching television, surfing the web, or occasionally at conventions or on city streets, people must decide "Just who are these celebrities and how (if at all) should I react to them?" Celebrities too must interpret their own thoughts, feelings, and actions, as well as those of their fans, critics, co-workers, and interviewers. Virtually any topic or venue related to celebrity can be approached just as another occasion for meaning-making via social interaction.

Consider fans who wait in line for 30 minutes to obtain an autograph from an aging actor associated with a defunct television show. These fans may (or may not) view the occasion as a thrilling or nerve-wracking experience; they may note and commit to memory (for future story-telling) the star's every word and facial expression. A non-fan, of course, may wonder why anyone would pay money and stand in line to have a short, potentially awkward interaction with a "has been." Its meaning is not inherent. And what applies to staged encounters also applies to unexpected celebrity sightings. A fan who sees their favorite soap opera star in the supermarket may regard the experience as an unforgettable moment—a profound brush with greatness. Or, the star's casual sweat-pants and aloof facial expression may lead the fan to be "disappointed," "sad," or even "offended." Meanwhile, a nearby shopper may glance at and recognize the same celebrity but not care much at all.

Celebrities, too, must create and act on interpretations of ambiguous circumstances. Recall the example of Armin Shimerman ("Quark" from Star Trek: Deep Space Nine) from Chapter 2. Shimerman reportedly cut his autograph signing short after an over-eager fun lunged at him. But that sort of reaction is not automatic. Celebrities must decide: Are fans' actions threatening or simply enthusiastic? Was this fan's behavior just a fluke, or should all fans now be defined as potential threats? How should I define and act toward those "intimate strangers" who approach me in public?

In short, our interactional approach to celebrity and fame is to focus on dilemmas of meaning and patterns of interpretation and interaction. This is a somewhat minimalist orientation, in that we eschew grand narratives that place celebrity and fame into a larger analytical story about class conflict, the commercialization of social life, the spread of narcissism, and other woeful (but potentially informative) tales. This minimalism has its strengths and weaknesses, as no viewpoint is perfect. While we can easily be criticized for neglecting some larger structural contexts, we can perhaps be appreciated for our attempt to understand behavior from the point of view of those who are interacting. We have done our best to avoid imposing (in a hasty, confident manner) a foreign viewpoint onto celebrities and fans, as sometimes happens when scholars become engrossed with larger theoretical, moral, or political agendas.

Microstructuralism

Part of "focusing on the meanings people live by" involves being sensitive to the understandings and moralities that operate in specific social interactions. Seeing things from the "participants" perspectives requires understanding their notions of right/wrong, normal/abnormal, routine/non-routine, and so on, rather than simply imposing our own.

In *Stargazing*, we have followed a long tradition in Sociology of searching for the social norms that (to some degree) shape and regulate social interaction. Just as there are written laws that tell us how to behave, there are unwritten and informal rules for virtually all aspects of our behavior: our clothing, our eating habits, our friendships, and so on. Sometimes Americans assume that certain behaviors are only "natural"—for example, that women tend to wear their hair longer than men or that men avoid wearing skirts, that we eat cow muscle but not dogs or worms, that (perhaps) forming dozens of "friendships" on Facebook is fine while 500 is excessive. But the pursuit of "acceptable" behaviors (and the sanctioning of deviance) is shaped by cultural understandings, by norms that are created by groups and internalized by individuals. What seems merely "logical" to us is actually socio-logical. In some cultures dogs and worms are considered food, and long hair and kilts are defined as masculine.

Sociologists delight in discovering that some unexplored or taken-for-granted area of social life is actually subject to pervasive governance by social norms. For example, Hochschild (1983) famously drew attention to the fact that our emotional reactions are not merely biological sensations but are guided by cultural convention. We judge people negatively if they feel the *wrong type* of feeling (e.g., amusement rather than sadness at a funeral), or even if they express the right feeling *with too much or too little intensity* (e.g., being extraordinarily nervous about a short class assignment or giving a bored "yeah, whatever" response to a sincere wedding proposal). Similarly, other social scientists have found norms governing even the most "wild" or "animalistic" events, such as soccer riots (Marsh, Rosser, and Harre 1978) or drunken behavior (MacAndrew and Edgerton 1969).

Goffman is most famous for drawing attention to the seemingly-infinite number of interactional rules and rituals that shape our daily lives. In virtually all social situations, he argued, human beings felt some pressure to "fit in":

> The words one applies to a child on his first trip to a restaurant presumably hold for everyone all the time: the individual must be 'be good' and not cause a scene or a disturbance. . . . He [or she] must keep within the spirit . . . of the situation; he must not be . . . out of place. (Goffman 1963:11)

For Goffman, conforming to the demands of situations involves playing a context-specific role that shapes our sense of self. We are judged by others and by ourselves as we succeed or fail in obeying norms and performing these roles.

> . . . [T]he individual must see to it that the impressions of him that are conveyed in the situation are compatible with role-appropriate personal qualities effectively imputed to him: a judge is supposed to be deliberate and sober; a pilot, in a cockpit, to be cool; a

bookkeeper to be accurate and neat in doing his work. These personal qualities . . . provide a basis of self-image for the incumbent and a basis for the image that . . . others will have of him. A self, then, virtually awaits the individual entering a position; he need only conform to the pressures on him and he will find a *me* ready-made for him. (Goffman 1961, pp. 87-88)

In Chapters 2 and 3, we followed this microstructuralist tradition by examining the norms governing encounters with celebrities. Recall those *pre-staged encounters* where fans wait in line for a brief interaction with—and possibly an autograph or photograph from—a star. In these encounters, interaction is highly circumscribed and predictable. Where fans stand and the kinds of demands they can place on celebrities (in terms of time, physical contact, etc.) are fairly obvious and sometimes explicit. Convention staff may make announcements and set up rope lines; neophyte fans may observe those earlier in line, to get a sense of the sort of interaction they should anticipate and the limits to which they can push their encounters with the famous. Security is often present to maintain boundaries should a fan be tempted to deviate (e.g., by asking for too much time, too many autographs, or too much physical contact from a star).

Unlike staged encounters, *celebrity sightings* are serendipitous meetings that occur between fans and the famous in public. These events are relatively rare and unexpected, with (one might assume) few or no guidelines. Yet the data from Chapter 2 showed that respondents held common understandings of appropriate behavior even in these situations. Random celebrity sightings are, to some degree, norm-governed too. The expectations for "how to interact with celebrities" seem to derive from more mundane expectations about the treatment of non-acquaintances in public settings.

Goffman (1963:84) argued that a rule of "civil inattention" seemed to regulate a huge swath of social interaction in society. In everyday life, we notice but usually do not engage strangers as we walk past them on the sidewalk, sit at a nearby table in a restaurant, or ride an elevator. We do not ignore strangers to the point that we would bump into them; however, we do not invade their privacy by staring at them or initiating a conversation without some good reason.

Adherence to the norm of civil inattention is not always an easy task. The strength of people's compliance can be put to the test "whenever someone of divergent social status or very divergent physical appearance is present" (Goffman 1963:84). Just as it could be difficult not to stare at a person who has an amputated arm or a disfigured face, it can be difficult to purposefully neglect a famous (or infamous) stranger who has entered our presence. This is especially true when the "stranger" is someone whose work we know a great deal about and are highly fond of.

In the data we analyzed in Chapters 2 and 3, the most common pattern in celebrity sightings was for fans to feign non-recognition. When a fan of Snoop Dogg saw the rapper in the airport, it was difficult to pretend he didn't notice the celebrity, but she did it anyway out of a sense of obligation. "I had a difficult time not staring at [Snoop] and the girls he was with," she reported. "I tried to play it cool, and not make a big deal of the situation." Some respondents tried to alert their companions to a celebrity sighting without giving any obvious indication that they had witnessed a celebrity. A self-described "huge fan" of soap opera star Wally Kurth subtly pointed out the actor to her father "in a manner that it wouldn't be obvious" because she "just didn't want to bother [Kurth], or disturb him in his private life." Other respondents waited until the celebrity had left the scene before commenting on the sighting to their friends or relatives.

Even when fans reported approaching celebrities, their accounts were still oriented to the norm of civil inattention. One fan saw Vince Vaughan in a restaurant and interrupted him to ask for a photograph. She tried to excuse her behavior by telling the actor "Sorry, you are probably really sick of this, but no one would believe me if I told them I met you!" Fans also seemed to judge celebrities' behavior with civil inattention in mind. Celebrities who drew attention to themselves—for example, by wearing overly-contrived disguises or by interacting loudly with their entourage—made it difficult for fans to ignore them and hence were judged as behaving inappropriately. Thus, we argued that there is a moral order governing celebrity sightings, as fleeting and rare as these encounters may be.

Negotiated Order

Microstructuralists convincingly argue that there are norms governing nearly every aspect of our behavior: how **LOUD** or quietly we talk, what we wear and eat, whom we date, and on and on. Even uncommon and extraordinary encounters, such as celebrity sightings, can be guided by informal norms.

Yet, as ubiquitous and influential as interactional norms can be, it is possible to overstate the degree to which they "govern" our lives. In fact, the very pervasiveness of norms raises the possibility that people must make active efforts to "balance" or "navigate" between competing expectations in certain situations. For example, students who receive an "A" on a difficult exam may need to harmonize their conflicting desires to celebrate their success, to conform to teachers' expectations about classroom decorum, and to appear appropriately sympathetic to other classmates who scored poorly.

Along with microstructuralism, we have applied the "negotiated order" lens in *Stargazing*, in order to highlight the contradictory and emergent properties of situations and norms.[2] In particular, Chapters 3 and 4 devoted much attention to the work people put into creating a somewhat spontaneous and multi-faceted experience of "what is going on" at any given moment.

The view that social interaction has a "negotiated order" has been applied to many different areas of social life, such as amusement and humor, exotic dancing, nightclub behavior, and the dangers of bicycling on city streets.[3] Perhaps the most famous example is Emerson's (reprinted in 2006) classic study of gynecological exams. For doctors and nurses, this exam is just another routine medical procedure that they have performed hundreds of times. The patients, on the other hand, are inclined to view the exam as an unusual and intimate situation. Which definition of the encounter is right? Each interpretation of the encounter calls for different, potentially contradictory emotions and actions. Emerson argued that the medical staff needed to negotiate with patients a "balance" between these two competing understandings—though the balance was usually tilted toward the medical interpretation. Doctors (at this time, primarily male) would use somewhat detached language ("the vagina" not "your vagina") while speaking in a nonchalant tone of voice, avoiding eye contact, and wearing the obligatory white lab coat. All of these can be seen as strategies for promoting the dominant medical definition of the situation, along with its accompanying norms— especially that patients should submit to this routine medical procedure in a relaxed, cooperative fashion.

At the same time, Emerson noted, the doctors would take subtle steps to acknowledge the patients' understanding of the situation—the subordinate definition of the situation. The doctor "admitted" that the exam was an unusual and intimate encounter by referring to the patient by her first name (rather than "patient X"), completing tasks in a brisk but gentle fashion, and keeping the patient's body largely covered so that nudity was minimized. Patients could affect the "balance" in many ways. Patients who tended to express much embarrassment in their actions and demeanor, and could not relax, might cause the doctor to adjust his actions and thereby move the encounter towards the patients' definition of the situation. The doctor (and his nursing staff) might take extra time to establish rapport or adopt an especially soothing tone of voice. On the other hand, the doctor might counter the patient's actions with continued nonchalance, in an effort to "hold the line" and continue to define the encounter as a routine medical procedure.

Similar "balancing" acts can be seen across a wide range of situations. Consider two college students who get together for a study session the weekend before an exam. Throughout the occasion, the participants must negotiate some balance between the contradictory definitions that "This is a work-related gathering" and "This is a personal and sociable encounter." If one participant makes a humorous comment, it can be seen as a "proposal" to move the situation in a more sociable direction. The other student's reactions would then represent their "counter-offers" as they negotiate the emerging definitions and norms of the situation: for example, they might laugh loudly and contribute their own jokes or anecdotes, or they might smile tersely and then draw attention back to the task at hand. With these sorts of subtle (and sometimes not-so-subtle!) maneuvers, college students negotiate a balance between sociability and "just business" in their study sessions.

Parallel negotiations might be found when grocery clerks greet shoppers, when barbers cut their clients' hair, when politicians give interviews to journalists, and other situations.

Encounters that involve celebrity and fame can also be analyzed through the lens of negotiated order, using data from this book. Recall from Chapter 3 the example of a fan spotting Magic Johnson working out at the gym. In this celebrity sighting, a trainer acted as a go-between, informing the fan that it was OK to say "hello" to Magic but not to ask for an autograph. Still, within these parameters, there is much room for negotiation. For example, how long will the "hello" last? Will the interaction be warm and friendly or cold and perfunctory? Arguably, fans can look to stars for cues and vice versa. An excited tone of voice on the part of the fan can act as an "opening bid" that sets the potential level of sociability high. In response, Magic could have waived the fan off, or perhaps nodded hello with a brief and toothless smile, as a way to steer the interaction "downward." On the other hand, Magic could have stepped off the treadmill, given the fan a sweaty bear-hug, and said "I love to meet fans! Tell me about yourself! Are you from L.A.? Were you always a big Lakers fan?" These options would likely embolden the fan and push the sociability "upward." As we reported, though, Magic took a middle path and gave the fan a handshake and a jovial "high five" while continuing to exercise on the treadmill. Like Emerson's (2006) doctors, perhaps Magic wanted to keep the fan happy by encouraging or allowing *some* intimacy, but not *too* much intimacy. (We would expect that shy or reticent fans [like gynecology patients] can perhaps be given more warmth and attention, whereas eager fans can be greeted with a more distant tone, to negotiate and encourage the right balance.)

In Chapter 4, we explicitly adopted and pursued a more complicated extension of the negotiated order perspective via Goffman's notion of *frame analysis.*[4] There we saw impersonators and their audiences balancing several frames (or layers of understandings) regarding "what is going on" in the show. Who is on stage? Exactly who is addressing the audience? Is it the impersonator, the celebrity being impersonated, the character in the song that is being sung, or someone else? Impersonators and their audiences seem well aware that there are competing frames at

hand, but this does not undermine the show. Rather, subtly acknowledging the contradictory layers is part of the fun—as long as performer
and audience are both willing and effective collaborators.

We compared impersonators' performances to games, a metaphor
that highlights rule-governed activity to be sure. However, participants
in the game of celebrity-impersonation can play both *within* and *with*
the rules. There are some limits to what the impersonators and the
audience members can do, but there is also much discretion in which
layers of reality and fantasy they choose to attend to, and how they
behave within those frames. For example, many of the most popular
celebrities impersonated are no longer alive, which means that the game
only works if no one stands up and shouts, "But wait—you can't be Elvis.
He's dead!" However, there are ways to make furtive reference to the fact
that the impersonator is not the real Elvis—and both impersonator and
audience may do so, as long as they don't cross the line or take it too far.
Lighthearted reminders of the performance's unreality are workable; an
Elvis impersonator may strategically reveal that he has visited the King's
grave at Graceland, then seconds later act as if he were the King himself,
who was in turn performing a character from a song (e.g., the lovelorn
man in "Heartbreak Hotel"). So, the show provides a setting in which
Elvis can be both dead (the real Elvis, at least) and alive (as embodied by
the Elvis impersonator). Outside of that occasion, Elvis is simply dead,
and anyone who acts as if he's not is suspect; in other settings, those who
believe Elvis is alive ("he's been hiding") are often seen as a bit peculiar,
out of touch with reality, or even crazy.

Discourse Analysis

The "microstructuralist" perspective imagines individuals moving amid
a maze of predefined situations and norm-governed behaviors. The
"negotiated order" perspective highlights the emergent nature of norms
and people's ability to interactively balance flexible and competing
understandings of the same situation. Both perspectives build on the
premise that meaning is not inherent. In microstructuralism, our behavior
is judged "appropriate" or "inappropriate" depending on culturally variable norms that are (arguably) more socio-logical than they are logical. In

negotiated order, multiple and conflicting definitions of "what is going on" are managed and enacted by the participants of social settings.

Another lens we have used in our book, and a common focus in the sociology of interaction, combines the premise that "meaning is not inherent" with a strict attention to the discursive processes by which some semblance of order is given to our lives. There are many varieties of discourse analysis, but for our purposes we emphasize some sociologists' tendency to treat all *descriptions* as interpretive *claims*. Since any supposed *thing*—any object, person, behavior, situation—can be characterized in different ways, one route for interactional research is to focus on how those *things* come into and out of existence via people's talk.

Discourse analysis often involves a careful "bracketing" of the phenomena in question, so that researchers refrain from presuming any particular definition of them. For example, there is a rich tradition of research in sociology that treats social problems as claims-making rather than as objective conditions (Best 2008). These scholars do not necessarily deny that there may be something "real" to putative problems like attention deficit disorder, drunk driving, marital inequality, school shootings, global warming, or other issues of concern. But they do argue that any supposed condition can be characterized in number of different ways, and these interpretations shape our reactions (on personal, group, or governmental levels). Consequently, discourse analysts make it a priority to examine a range of claims-making about social problems, usually without presuming to know or trying to determine the ultimate truth of the matter (Holstein and Miller 2003; Loseke 1999).

A discursive scholar might be interested in, say, divergent religious narratives about global warming. Perhaps s/he would find that members of some spiritual communities portray global warming as insignificant compared to other-worldly concerns (such as heaven and hell and the coming return of a savior), whereas other religious individuals or groups discussed global warming as a preventable sin (since human beings are allowing God's creation to be abused). A discourse analyst would not set out to prove whether either story was true; instead, s/he would document the diversity of those tales and study them as two of many options for making sense of apparent changes in the climate.

In *Stargazing*, we applied a discursive lens to our data, though (in Chapters 5 and 6) we focused on assertions about "inner" bodily conditions rather than on assertions about major societal problems. People sometimes assume that "what we think and feel" are relatively simple matters, but these issues are arguably discussed and debated as much as any politically-charged problem is (see Harris 2010). Mental and emotional descriptions can be profitably studied as interpretive claims-making, as others before us have noted (Gubrium 2003; Staske 1996).

Stars sometimes use the formulaic expression "I'm happy to be here" to characterize their feelings. Celebrities may invoke that common phrase in front of millions of viewers on the red carpet, while we may do so upon arriving at a friend's party or at a job interview with a prospective employer. Whether the setting is extraordinary or mundane, one can view the description of "happy" as an interpretation (and potentially a strategic one) rather than a simple reality report. Happiness can be critically interrogated, should we choose to do so. How does the person know that s/he is feeling happy? Is this the whole truth, or are they feeling other emotions (e.g., nervousness) as well? Would they characterize their emotions differently if the audience and/or context were different? Is the description perhaps as much goal-oriented (e.g., creating a positive impression on others) as it is a careful and honest reflection on their supposed emotional state? These sorts of questions tend to encourage us to view emotional descriptions as ways of constructing meaning and influencing social interaction.

Now consider cognition. In everyday life we are often asked to be honest and say what we *really* think, to check the survey box that best represents our feelings or attitudes, and so on. But if meaning is not inherent, and if any *thing* can be described in many ways, then "what we think" can also be approached as a discursive interpretation. Stars, like the rest of us, may claim they "always knew" or "can't believe" something. For example, on the red carpet, an actor may assert that he "always knew" his movie would be popular with audiences, just as we might claim that we "always knew" we would be a business major or a doctor or something else. An actress may exclaim that she "can't believe" how incredible someone's dress is, just as we may pronounce our incredulity in a companion's behavior ("I can't believe you did that!"). With some critical questioning and prodding, though, it seems at least possible (if not likely) that the tentativeness of these descriptions might become clear. Perhaps celebrities, just like ourselves, might revise "always knew" to "frequently suspected" or "often hoped," and "can't believe" could be replaced with "hard to believe" or more radically to "I guess it's not that out-of-the-ordinary after all"—especially if our primary goal switches from making a good impression to avoiding a controversy or fight.

In this manner, in Chapters 5 and 6, we invoked and applied the lens of discourse analysis to show how celebrities' thoughts and feelings, like our own mundane experiences, can be treated as linguistic social constructions. We all inherit concepts and slogans from our culture, which we use (with others' collaboration or resistance) in a context-sensitive way to make meaning and guide conduct.

Final Thoughts/Caveats

In *Stargazing*, we have applied a range of lenses to our data, in order to demonstrate and promote interactional, meaning-centered analyses of celebrity and fame. We think the traditions discussed here are at least a good starting point, and can bear much intellectual fruit. However, it is important for us to admit—and for readers and future researchers to keep in mind—that it is impossible to focus on everything at once.

In some places in this book we have emphasized microstructuralist concerns (e.g., Chapters 2 and 3), while in other places we draw more extensively from either the perspective of negotiated order (e.g., Chapter 4) or the tradition of discourse analysis (e.g., Chapters 5 and 6). We are tempted to argue that we have let the data dictate which perspective is most relevant. This is an attractive possibility; it is almost relaxing and reassuring to conceive of our task as merely "discerning" the truth rather than "making" it. However, such an orientation stands in tension with the fundamental premise of interactionism—that meaning is not inherent. If anything can be interpreted in multiple ways, we must admit that the "sense" we make of our data is itself, to a large extent, something we *construct* rather than simply *find*.

Perhaps the best approach, then, is to not settle on a single orientation. We can try to let the data "tell us" which perspective is most relevant, but we can also purposefully switch between lenses in order to
see if we can learn something new and interesting about social
interaction—whether in our daily lives or in the world of celebrity.

We encourage readers and celebrity researchers alike to do that.
Interactionist perspectives and concepts are most interesting and useful
when they can be applied creatively to a wide range of settings and
behaviors. By bringing tried-and-true interactionist traditions to bear
on celebrity and fame, we can draw connections between a fascinating
array of ordinary and extraordinary realms. This would advance interactionist theory, and could give pop-culture aficionados some deeper and
more critical ways of consuming the media's bountiful coverage of
celebrity and fame.

NOTES

1 The Sociology of Celebrity

1. We will use fame and celebrity somewhat interchangeably in this book, mostly because there are so many different usages of each term in the literature. Different studies include many different categories of people under the heading of celebrity—rock stars, movie actors, athletes, supermodels, politicians, literary and religious icons all get the celebrity treatment from scholars. However, many researchers do attempt to "operationalize" their usages of these terms and to distinguish them from one another in some way. The consensus distinction seems to be both temporal and substantive: fame is seen as the more enduring quality, while celebrity might just be a flash in the pan—"fame without history," Braudy calls it (1986:599). And fame endures because of its greater substance; it is likely to be based in *bona fide* achievement of some sort, while celebrities are merely "well known for [their] well-knownness" (Boorstin 1961:57). Though the meanings may differ, together fame and celebrity constitute a unified field of inquiry.

2 The Dynamics of Fan–Celebrity Relations

1. See Emerson, Ferris, and Gardner (1998); Lowney and Best (1995); Zona, Sharma, and Lane (1993).
2. Most of the fans interviewed were female. The racial-ethnic makeup of the group was five African American women, one Latina woman, nine Anglo women, two Latino men, one Asian man, and two Anglo men, and all respondents ranged in age from 22 to 25. All of the interview respondents were employed in white-collar, technical, or professional fields, and about half of them were married and/or had children. One of the single Latino men was openly gay. Each of the respondents belonged to one or more groups of active television fans, and their other affiliations included various churches, athletic groups, charitable organizations, and professional associations. In other words, by standard sociological measures of social anchorage, none of the respondents had the profile of a social isolate (see Bellah et al. 1996; Putnam 1995).
3. Or could it be that the actor wants to know the fans' names so that he can protect himself from them in the future?

3 Seeing and Being Seen

1. See, respectively, Davis (1991), Dordick (1997), Duneier (1999), Lenney and Sercombe (2002), Longhurst (2001), Persson (2001), and Robins, Sanders, and Cahill (1991).

143

2. See Adler and Adler (1989); Braudy (1986); Brown (1999); Caughey (1984); Ferris (2001); Gamson (1994); Horton and Wohl (1956); Schickel (1985).

3. It can also be interpreted as a version of Goffman's "parade-ground decorum" (1974:204), in which out-of-frame activity is disattended to avoid the collapse of the entire frame.

4. Risks to fans from celebrity encounters are not merely reputational. In 2001, a fan sued actor Don Johnson for sexual battery, assault, and emotional distress (*Los Angeles Times* 2001, F2). The petitioner claimed that she noticed Johnson in a San Francisco sushi bar and approached him, intending to introduce herself as a fan. Upon making her introduction, the fan claims Johnson accosted her, groping her and making lewd comments (no information on this case's disposition is available). In addition, paparazzi, who may not be fans but who by virtue of their occupation are professional celebrity stalkers, have been battered by celebrities who feel their privacy is invaded by photographers, even when they are in public places. These assaults were regularly broadcast on E! Television's program *Celebrities Uncensored* (2003–2004) and can now be viewed on *TMZ*.

5 "How does it Feel to be a Star?"

1. This epigraph is taken from a 2005 interview conducted by The Associated Press.
2. See Harris (2010) for a longer review.
3. See Staske (1996) on upgrading and downgrading attributions of emotion.
4. Video broadcasts, however, sometimes catch interviewers looking at cue cards or reading off index cards that may serve as "cheat sheets," providing information about each star as they arrive at the interview station.
5. The transcripts were analyzed using grounded theory methods. They were first coded for all mentions of emotion—anytime a celebrity or interviewer used a phrase or term associated with an emotion, that utterance was flagged. We coded both for explicit emotion terms (like "Don't you <u>love</u> this?" or "I'm <u>nervous</u>"), as well as for less explicit remarks (such as "I feel like <u>I'm being embraced by the entire industry</u>") that were emotional in tone and reference nonetheless. These pieces of coded data were then grouped with similar others as part of a more focused coding process, in order to discern more detailed patterns in red-carpet emotion-talk.
6. The phrase "conflict diamonds" refers to diamonds that were mined in a war zone for the purposes of funding military activity—a topic of the movie "Blood Diamonds."
7. See Fraser and Brown (2002), Kellner (2001), and Lines (2001).

6 "When did you Know that you'd be a Star?"

1. This interest can also be seen in popular culture media—television shows, magazines, newspapers, fan sites—where commentators speculate about whether celebrities have fallen in or out of love, are jealous about an old flame's new relationship, are angry about another celebrity's behavior, and so on.
2. For example, see Brekhus (2007), Callero (1991), Meltzer (2003), Smith (1982), and Zerubavel (1997).
3. See, respectively, Antaki (2004), Edwards (1997), Lynch and Bogen (2005) and Puchta and Potter (2002).
4. It seems likely that such celebrities would also make themselves available for interviews, rather than skipping the ceremony or entering the venue through a less public entrance.
5. Brigitte was an E! viewer who won a contest—"Ryan's Red Carpet Challenge"—which gave her the opportunity to interview a celebrity of her choice. Ryan Seacrest invited her on camera to perform the interview with Hugh Laurie.

7 Conclusion

1. A relatively recent development in the contemporary west (Brumberg 1998).
2. If microstructuralism portrays society as a pre-defined maze with firm walls to constrain our path, negotiated order conjures an image of an Amish barn-raising, where a group of collaborators pull on ropes to lift constraining walls of their own creation.
3. See Flaherty (1990), Kidder (2005), Lerum (2006) and Sanders (2005).
4. Readers should be warned that Goffman's treatise on frame analysis is known to be an especially difficult text that has been interpreted in many different ways (Denzin and Keller 1981).

REFERENCES

Adalian, J. 2009. "Kevin Burns: The Producer Next Door." In *TV Week Online*. http://www.tvweek.com/news/2009/06/kevin_burns_the_producer_next.php (accessed 9/19/09).

Adler, P. A. and P. Adler. 1989. "The Gloried Self: The Aggrandizement and the Constriction of Self." *Social Psychology Quarterly* 52(4):299-310.

Adorno, T. and M. Horkheimer. 1993. "The Culture Industry: Enlightenment as Mass Deception." Pp. 31–41 in *The Cultural Studies Reader*, edited by S. During. London: Routledge.

Antaki, C. 2004. "Reading Minds or Dealing with Interactional Implications?" *Theory & Psychology* 14:667-683.

Ashe, D. D. and L. E. McCutcheon. 2001. "Shyness, Loneliness and Attitude toward Celebrities." *Current Research in Social Psychology* 6:124-132.

Bacon-Smith, C. 1992. *Enterprising Women: Television Fandom and the Creation of Popular Myth*. Philadelphia, PA: University of Pennsylvania Press.

Barrett, L. F. 2006. "Solving the Emotion Paradox: Categorization and the Experience of Emotion." *Personality and Social Psychology Review* 10:20-46.

Baumgartner, M. P. 1988. *The Moral Order of a Suburb*. New York: Oxford Univeresity Press.

Bellah, R. N., R. Madsen, W. M. Sullivan, A. Swidler and S. M. Tipton. 1996. *Habits of the Heart: Individualism and Commitment in American Life*. Berkeley, CA: University of California Press.

Berger, P. 1963. *Invitation to Sociology*. Garden City, NY: Anchor Books.

Berger, P. L. and T. Luckmann. 1966. *The Social Construction of Reality: A Treatise in the Sociology of Knowledge*. Garden City, NY: Doubleday.

Best, J. 2008. *Social Problems*. New York: Norton.

Bielby, D. and C. L. Harrington. 1993. "Public Meanings, Private Screenings: The Formation of Social Bonds through the Televisual Experience." *Perspectives on Social Problems* 3:155-178.

Blumer, H. 1969. *Symbolic Interactionism*. Englewood Cliffs, NJ: Prentice-Hall.

———. 1981. "George Herbert Mead." Pp. 136-169 in *The Future of the Sociological Classics*, edited by B. Rhea. London: Allen and Unwin.

Boorstin, D. 1961. *The Image: A Guide to Pseudo-Events in America*. New York: Harper and Row.

Braudy, L. 1986. *The Frenzy of Renown: Fame and its History*. New York: Vintage Books.

Brekhus, W. H. 2007. "The Rutgers School: A Zerubavelian Culturalist Cognitive Sociology." *European Journal of Social Theory* 10:453-470.

Brown, B. C. 1999. *Kingship and the French Revolution of 1830: The Meaning of Royal Authority in Popular Political Culture and Orléanism*. Ph.D. dissertation, University of California, Santa Barbara, CA.

Brumberg, J. J. 1998. *The Body Project: An Intimate History of American Girls*. New York: Vintage.

Callero, P. L. 1991. "Toward a Sociology of Cognition." Pp. 43-54 in *The Self-Society Dynamic: Cognition, Emotion, and Action*, edited by J. A. Howard and P. L. Callero. New York: Cambridge University Press.

Cashmore, E. 2006. *Celebrity Culture*. London, UK: Routledge.

Caughey, J. L. 1984. *Imaginary Social Worlds: A Cultural Approach*. Lincoln, NE: University of Nebraska Press.

Davis, K. 2006 [1947]. "Final Note on a Case of Extreme Isolation." Pp. 89-95 in *The Production of Reality*, 4th ed., edited by J. O'Brien. Thousand Oaks, CA: Pine Forge.

Davis, P. 1991. "Stranger Intervention into Child Punishment in Public Places." *Social Problems* 38(2):227-46.

Denzin, N. and C. Keller. 1981. "Frame Analysis Reconsidered." *Contemporary Sociology* 10(1):52-60.

Dordick, G. A. 1997. *Something Left to Lose: Personal Relations and Survival among New York's Homeless*. Philadelphia, PA: Temple.

Dugdale, T. 2000. "The Fan and (Auto)Biography: Writing the Self in the Stars." *Journal of Mundane Behavior* 1(2): www.mundanebehavior.org.

Duneier, M. 1999. *Sidewalk*. New York: Farrar, Strauss and Giroux.

Edwards, D. 1997. *Discourse and Cognition*. London, UK: Sage.

——. 1999. "Emotion Discourse." *Culture and Psychology* 5(3):271-291.

Edwards, D. and Potter, J. 2005. "Discursive Psychology, Mental States and Descriptions." Pp. 241-259 in *Conversation and Cognition*, edited by H. te Molder and J. Potter. New York: Cambridge University Press.

Ehrenreich, B. 1990. "Star Dreck." Pp. 26–29 in *The Worst Years of Our Lives: Irreverent Notes from a Decade of Greed*. New York: Pantheon Books.

Ellis, C. 1986. *Fisher Folk: Two Communities on Chesapeake Bay*. Lexington, KY: University Press of Kentucky.

Emerson, J. 1970. "Nothing Unusual Is Happening." Pp. 208-222 in *Human Nature and Collective Behavior: Papers in Honor of Herbert Blumer*, edited by T. Shibutani. Englewood Cliffs, NJ: Prentice Hall.

——. 2006 [1970]. "Behavior in Private Places: Sustaining Definitions of Reality in Gynecological Examinations." Pp. 201-214 in *The Production of Reality, 4th ed.*, edited by J. O'Brien. Thousand Oaks, CA: Pine Forge.

Emerson, R. M., K. O. Ferris, and C. B. Gardner. 1998. "On Being Stalked." *Social Problems* 45(3):289-314.

Emerson, R. M., R. I. Fretz, and L. L. Shaw. 1995. *Writing Ethnographic Fieldnotes*. Chicago, IL: Chicago University Press.

Evans, N. 1998. "Games of Hide and Seek: Race, Gender and Drag in 'The Crying Game' and 'The Birdcage'." *Text & Performance Quarterly* 18:199-215.

Ferris, K. O. 2001. "Through a Glass Darkly: The Dynamics of Fan-Celebrity Encounters." *Symbolic Interaction* 24(1):25-47.

——. 2004. "Seeing and Being Seen: The Moral Order of Celebrity Sightings." *Journal of Contemporary Ethnography* 33(3):236-264

——. 2007a. "The Sociology of Celebrity." *Sociology Compass* 1(1):371-384.

——. 2007b. "Ain't Nothing Like the Real Thing, Baby: Celebrity Impersonators and Their Audiences." *Text & Performance Quarterly* 30(1):60-80.

Flaherty, M. G. 1984. "A Formal Approach to the Study of Amusement in Social Interaction." *Studies in Symbolic Interaction* 5:71-82.

——. 1990. "Two Conceptions of the Social Situation: Some Implications of Humor." *Sociological Quarterly* 31:93-106.

Fox, K. J. 2001. "Self-Change and Resistance in Prison." Pp. 176-192 in *Institutional Selves: Troubled Identities in a Postmodern World*, edited by J. F. Gubrium and J. A. Holstein. New York: Oxford University Press.

Fraser, B. P. and W. J. Brown. 2002. "Media, Celebrities and Social Influence: Identification with Elvis Presley." *Mass Communication and Society* 5:183-206.

Friedman, D. and C. Buck. 2006. "Where's Michael?" *Gentleman's Quarterly* (May issue).

Gabler, N. 1999. *Life the Movie: How Entertainment Conquered Reality*. New York: Alfred A. Knopf.

Gamson, J. 1994. *Claims to Fame: Celebrity in Contemporary America*. Berkeley, CA: University of California Press.

Gardner, C. B. 1988. "Access Information: Public Lies and Private Peril." *Social Problems* 35:384–397.

——. 1998. *Passing by: Gender and Public Harassment*. Berkeley, CA: University of California Press.

Gilbert, T. 2009. "'Kourtney and Khloe' Season Finale a High for E!". *TV Week Online.* http://www.tvweek.com/blogs/tvbizwire/2009/10/kourtney-khloe-season-finale-t.php (accessed 9/19/09).

Gitlin, T. 1998. "The Culture of Celebrity." *Dissent* 45:81-83.

Glaser, B. G. and A. L. Strauss. 1967. *The Discovery of Grounded Theory: Strategies for Qualitative Research*. New York: Aldine de Gruyter.

Goffman, E. 1959. *The Presentation of Self in Everyday Life*. New York: Doubleday.

——. 1961. *Encounters: Two Studies in the Sociology of Interaction*. Indianapolis, IN: Bobbs-Merrill Educational Publishing.

——. 1963. *Behavior in Public Places: Notes on the Social Organization of Gatherings*. New York: Free Press.

——. 1967. *Interaction Ritual: Essays on Face-to-Face Behavior*. New York: Anchor.

——. 1974. *Frame Analysis: An Essay on the Organization of Experience*. New York: Harper and Row.

Goldsmith, J. 2006. "People who Need People: Sucking Up to Celebs Builds Mag as TW Money Machine." *Variety* (July 9).

Greenberg, D. 2001. "Familiar Faces." *Los Angeles Business Journal* (April 23).

Gubrium, J. F. 1989. "Emotion Work and Emotive Discourse in the Alzheimer's Disease Experience." *Current Perspectives on Aging and the Life Cycle* 5:243-268.

——. 1992. *Out of Control: Family Therapy and Domestic Disorder*. Newbury Park, CA: Sage.

——. 2003 [1986]. "The Social Preservation of Mind: The Alzheimer's Disease Experience." Pp. 180-190 in *Inner Lives and Social Worlds: Readings in Social Psychology*, edited by J. A. Holstein and J. F. Gubrium. New York: Oxford University Press.

Gubrium, J. F. and J. A. Holstein. 1990. *What is Family?* Mountain View, CA: Mayfield.

——. 1995. "Qualitative Inquiry and the Deprivatization of Experience." *Qualitative Inquiry* 1:204-222.

Hackett, L. 2007. "Inside People." People.com Archive 67(10). (March 12)

Halpern, J. 2007. *Fame Junkies: The Hidden Truths behind America's Favorite Addiction*. Boston, MA: Houghton-Mifflin.

Harris, S. R. 2010. *What Is Constructionism? Navigating Its Use in Sociology*. Boulder, CO: Lynne Rienner.

Harris, S. R. and K. O. Ferris (2009). "How Does It Feel to Be a Star? Identifying Emotion on the Red Carpet." *Human Studies* 32(3):133-152.

Heritage, J. 1984. *Garfinkel and Ethnomethodology*. Cambridge, UK: Polity Press.

Hochschild, A. R. 1983. *The Managed Heart: Commercialization of Human Feeling*. Berkeley, CA: University of California Press.

Holstein, J. A., and G. Miller. 2003. "Social Constructionism and Social Problems Work." Pp. 70-91 in *Challenges and Choices: Constructionist Perspectives on Social Problems*, edited by J. A. Holstein and G. Miller. New York: Aldine de Gruyter.

Horton, D. and R. R. Wohl. 1956. "Mass Communication and Para-Social Interaction: Observations on Intimacy at a Distance." *Psychiatry* 19(3):215-230.

Huppke, R. 2009. "Michael Jackson Impersonator Busier Than Ever as Act Morphs into Tribute". *Chicago Tribune*, August 29.

Irvine, L. 2008. "Animals and Sociology." *Sociology Compass* 2:1954-1971.

Jenkins, H. 1992. *Textual Poachers: Television Fans and Participatory Culture*. New York: Routledge.

Kaminer, W. 2005. "Get a Life: Illusions of Self-Invention." *The Hedgehog Review* 7(1):47-58.

Kellner, D. 2001. "The Sports Spectacle, Michael Jordan and Nike: Unholy Alliance?" Pp. 37-63 in *Michael Jordan, Inc.: Corporate Sport, Media Culture, and Late Modern America*, edited by D. L. Andrews. Albany, NY: SUNY Press.

Kidder, J. 2005. "Style and Action: A Decoding of Bike Messenger Symbols." *Journal of Contemporary Ethnography* 34(3):344-367.

King, B. 1992. "Stardom and Symbolic Degeneracy: Television and the Transformation of the Stars as Public Symbols." *Semiotica* 1:1-47.

Klapp, O. E. 1949. "Hero Worship in America." *American Sociological Review* 14:53-62.

Kollock, P. 1999. "The Economies of Online Cooperation: Gifts and Public Goods in Cyberspace." Pp. 220-239 in *Communities in Cyberspace*, edited by M. A. Smith and P. Kollock. London, UK: Routledge.

Lenney, M., and H. Sercombe. 2002. "'Did You See that Guy in the Wheelchair Down in the Pub?': Interactions across Difference in a Public Place." *Disability and Society* 17:5-18.

Lerum, K. 2006 [2001]. "'Precarious Situations' in a Strip Club: Exotic Dancers and the Problem of Reality Maintenance." Pp. 214-222 in *The Production of Reality*, 4th ed., edited by J. O'Brien. Thousand Oaks, CA: Pine Forge.

Liberman, K. L. 1999. "The Social Praxis of Communicating Meanings." *Text* 19:57-72.

Lines, G. 2001. "Villains, Fools or Heroes? Sports Stars as Role Models for Young People." *Leisure Studies* 20:285-303.

Lively, K. J. 2006. "Emotions in the Workplace." Pp. 569-590 in *Handbook of the Sociology of Emotions*, edited by J. H. Turner and J. E. Stets. New York: Springer.

Longhurst, R. 2001. "Breaking Corporeal Boundaries: Pregnant Bodies in Public Places." Pp. 81-94 in *Contested Bodies*, edited by R. Holliday and J. Hassard. London: Routledge.

Los Angeles Times. 2001. "Woman Sues Don Johnson." (July 14, F2)

Loseke, D. R. 1999. *Thinking about Social Problems: An Introduction to Constructionist Perspectives*. New York: Aldine de Gruyter.

Lowenthal, L. 1961. *Literature, Popular Culture, and Society*. Englewood Cliffs, NJ: Prentice-Hall.

Lowney, K. S. and J. Best. 1995. "Stalking Strangers and Lovers: Changing Media Typifications of a New Crime Problem." Pp. 33-57 in *Images of Issues: Typifying Contemporary Social Problems*, 2nd ed., edited by J. Best. New York: Aldine de Gruyter.

Lutz, C. A. 1988. *Unnatural Emotions: Everyday Sentiments on a Micronesian Atoll and their Challenges to Western Theory.* Chicago: University of Chicago Press.

Lynch, M. and D. Bogen. 2005. "'My Memory Has Been Shredded': A Non-Cognitivist Investigation of 'Mental' Phenomena." Pp. 226-240 in *Conversation and Cognition*, edited by H. te Molder and J. Potter. New York: Cambridge University Press.

MacAndrew, C. and R. B. Edgerton. 1969. *Drunken Comportment.* Chicago, IL: Aldine.

Maltby, J. and L. E. McCutcheon. 2001. "Correlations between Scores on Attitudes toward Celebrities and Authoritarianism." *Psychological Reports* 88:979-980.

Marcuse, H. 1991 [1964]. *One-Dimensional Man: Studies in the Ideology of Advanced Industrial Society.* Boston, MA: Beacon Press.

Marsh, P., E. Rosser, and R. Harre. 1978. *The Rules of Disorder.* London: Routledge and Kegan Paul.

Marshall, P. D. 1997. *Celebrity and Power: Fame in Contemporary Society.* Minneapolis, MN: University of Minnesota Press.

Matza, D. 1969. *Becoming Deviant.* Englewood Cliffs, NJ: Prentice Hall.

Maynard, D. W. 1991. "Goffman, Garfinkel, and Games." *Sociological Theory* 9(2):277-279.

McCutcheon, L. E. 2002. "Are Parasocial Relationship Styles Reflected in Love Styles?" *Current Research in Social Psychology* 7:82-93.

McCutcheon, L. E. and Maltby, J. 2002. "Personality Attributions about Individuals High and Low in the Tendency to Worship Celebrities." *Current Research in Social Psychology* 7: 325-338.

McCutcheon, L. E., R. Lange and J. Houran, 2002. "Conceptualization and Measurement of Celebrity Worship." *British Journal of Psychology* 93:67-87.

Mead, G. H. 1934. *Mind, Self, and Society.* Chicago, IL: Chicago University Press.

Meltzer, B. N. 2003. "Mind." Pp. 253-266 in *Handbook of Symbolic Interactionism*, edited by L. T. Reynolds and N. J. Herman-Kinney. Lanham, MD: Rowman and Littlefield.

Meyer, D. S. and J. Gamson. 1995. "The Challenge of Cultural Elites: Celebrities and Social Movements." *Sociological Inquiry* 65:181-206.

Mills, C. W. 1956. *The Power Elite.* New York: Oxford.

Monaco, J. 1978. *Celebrity.* New York: Delta.

O'Guinn, T. C. 1991. "Touching Greatness: The Central Midwest Barry Manilow Fan Club." Pp. 102-111 in *Highways and Buyways*, edited by R. W. Belk. Provo, UT: Association for Consumer Research.

People Magazine. 1994. December 12.

Persson, A. 2001. "Intimacy among Strangers: On Mobile Telephone Calls in Public Places." *Journal of Mundane Behavior* 2(3):309-316.

Peterson, G. 2006. "Cultural Theory and Emotions." Pp. 114-134 in *Handbook of the Sociology of Emotions*, edited by J. H. Turner and J. E. Stets. New York: Springer.

Postman, N. 1984. *Amusing Ourselves to Death.* New York: Viking.

Prus, R. 1996. *Symbolic Interaction and Ethnographic Research: Intersubjectivity and the Study of Human Lived Experience.* Albany, NY: SUNY Press.

Puchta, C. and J. Potter. 2002. "Manufacturing Individual Opinions: Market Research Focus Groups and the Discursive Psychology of Evaluation." *British Journal of Social Psychology* 41:345-363.

Putnam, R. D. 1995. "Bowling Alone: America's Declining Social Capital." *Journal of Democracy* 6(1):65-78.

Radelet M. L. and L. M. Roberts. 1983. "Parole Interviews of Sex Offenders: The Role of Impression Management." *Urban Life* 12(2):140-161.

Reid, E. 1999. "Hierarchy and Power: Social Control in Cyberspace." Pp. 107-133 in *Communities in Cyberspace*, edited by M. A. Smith and P. Kollock. London, UK: Routledge.

Robins, D. M., C. R. Sanders, and S. E. Cahill. 1991. "Dogs and their People: Pet-facilitated Interaction in a Public Setting." *Journal of Contemporary Ethnography* 20(1):3-25.

Robinson, B. "Jackson Impersonators Fear Molest Trial." ABCNews.com, January 28, 2004. http://abcnews.go.com/Entertainment/story?id=116579&page=1 (accessed September 3, 2010).

Rojek, C. 2001. *Celebrity*. London, UK: Reaktion Books.

Rosen, R. 1986. "Search for Yesterday." Pp. 42-67 in *Watching Television*, edited by T. Gitlin. New York: Pantheon Books.

Rosenberg, M. 1990. "Reflexivity and Emotions." *Social Psychology Quarterly* 53(1):3-12.

Russell, J. A. 1991. "Culture and the Categorization of Emotions." *Psychological Bulletin* 110:426-450.

Sanders, C. R. 2003a. "Actions Speak Louder than Words: Close Relationships between Humans and Nonhuman Animals." *Symbolic Interaction* 26:405-426.

——. 2003b. "Understanding Dogs: Caretakers' Attributions of Mindedness in Canine–Human Relationships." Pp. 191-201 in *Inner Lives and Social Worlds: Readings in Social Psychology*, edited by J. A. Holstein and J. F. Gubrium. New York: Oxford University Press.

——. 2007. "Mind, Self, and Human–Animal Joint Action." *Sociological Focus* 40(3):320-336.

Sanders, T. 2005. " 'It's Just Acting': Sex Worker's Strategies for Capitalizing on Sexuality." *Gender, Work and Organization* 12(4):319-342.

Scheppele, K. L. 1994. "Practices of Truth-Finding in a Court of Law: The Case of Revised Stories." Pp. 84-100 in *Constructing the Social*, edited by T. Sarbin and J. Kitsuse. London: Sage.

Schickel, R. 1985. *Intimate Strangers: The Culture of Celebrity*. New York: Fromm International.

Schutz, A. 1970. *On Phenomenology and Social Relations*. Chicago, IL: Chicago University Press.

Smith, A. D. 1999. "Problems of Conflict Management in Virtual Communities." Pp. 134-163 in *Communities in Cyberspace*, edited by M. A. Smith and P. Kollock. London, UK: Routledge.

Smith, C. W. 1982. "On the Sociology of Mind." Pp. 211-228 in *Explaining Human Behavior*, edited by P. Secord. Beverly Hills, CA: Sage.

Staske, S. A. 1996. "Talking Feelings: The Collaborative Construction of Emotion in Talk between Close Relational Partners." *Symbolic Interaction* 19(2):111-135.

Stebbins, R. A. 1980. " 'Amateur' and 'Hobbyist' as Concepts for the Study of Leisure Problems." *Social Problems* 27(4):413-417.

Stewart, J. 2003. "Where is Saddam?" 60 Minutes II. CBS. (Broadcast March 22)

Vannini, P. 2004. "The Meanings of a Star: Interpreting Pop Music Fans' Reviews." *Symbolic Interaction* 27:47-69.

Weber, M. 1966. "Class, Status and Party." Pp. 21-28 in *Class, Status and Power: Social Stratification in Comparative Perspective*, edited by R. Bendix and S. M. Lipset. New York: The Free Press.

——. 1968. *Economy and Society: An Outline of Interpretive Sociology*. New York: Bedminster Press.

West, D. 2005. "American Politics in the Age of Celebrity." *The Hedgehog Review* 7(1):59-65.

Young, S. M. and D. Pinsky. 2006. "Narcissism and Celebrity." *Journal of Research in Personality* 40:463-471.

Zerubavel, E. 1997. *Social Mindscapes: An Invitation to Cognitive Sociology*. Cambridge, MA: Harvard University Press.

Zona, M., K. K. Sharma, and J. Lane. 1993. "A Comparative Study of Erotomania and Obsessional Subjects in a Forensic Sample." *Journal of Forensic Sciences* 38:894-903.

SUBJECT INDEX

CELEBRITY INDEX